Imperium Press was founded in 2018 to supply students and laymen with works in the history of rightist thought. If these works are available at all in modern editions, they are rarely ever available in editions that place them where they belong: outside the liberal weltanschauung. Imperium Press' mission is to provide right thinkers with authoritative editions of the works that make up their own canon. These editions include introductions and commentary which place these canonical works squarely within the context of tradition, reaction, and counter-Enlightenment thought—the only context in which they can be properly understood.

UNDERSTANDING CONSPIRACY THEORIES

JOSH NEAL

Foreword by
Tyler Hamilton

PERTH
IMPERIUM PRESS
2024

Published by Imperium Press

www.imperiumpress.org

First Edition

A catalogue record for this book is available from the National Library of Australia

ISBN 978-1-923104-14-3 Paperback
ISBN 978-1-923104-15-0 Hardcover
ISBN 978-1-923104-16-7 E-book

Contents

Foreword

What was once was tucked away in the American outskirts of obscure talk radio, conventions populated by eccentrics, grainy VHS tapes, websites ostensibly offering hidden knowledge presented with kitsch graphics, and books placed next to the New Age and Esoteric sections of bookstores—the conspiracy theory—has gone from a dangerous curiosity to a mainstream banality. In the safety of the mainstream public imagination, through the assurance of credentialed experts, the conspiracy theorist was marginalized as a thoroughly irrational figure impervious to evidence and reason. In tandem, the conspiracy theory itself was mythologized through popular entertainment like *The X-Files*. As the conspiracy theory was simultaneously the object of ridicule and the object of fascination in the consciousness of American media, the resolute belief in the content of conspiracy theories became the lived reality for the fringe communities (and not necessarily uniform with one another) of doomsday cults, preppers, militias, and those choosing to reside in a southern compound. Throughout the 1960s to the mid-90s, clashes between the latter groups and both the mainstream of American life and government often led to instances of deadly violence. Concomitant with the social status of conspiracy theorists and the content of conspiracy theories, there is a natural connection with the trafficking of suspicion to political extremism. Our author, Josh Neal, has already provided us with an extensive and masterful treatment of political extremism in his previous work *American Extremist: The Psy-*

chology of Political Extremism. But we find ourselves having to deepen the analysis Josh already began.

The consciousness of the American public has taken a new turn towards the conspiracy theory, which is no longer the domain of a few curious social outcasts. The trafficking of suspicion has gone mainstream and not just among the often-accused populist right but in the everyday messaging of progressive media and politicians. Each side of the political aisle, in some ways deeply incommensurable with each other, shares the same urgent rhetoric proclaiming that the ascendancy of the other is not only some organized plan by manipulative ideologues to subvert the critical thinking capacity of the populace but a plan that will end in the destruction of the American way of life, liberty, and the pursuit of happiness. Our purpose is not to merely evaluate the truth-content of the now mainstream conspiracy theories, but to understand how suspicion became the norm in our political life and what should be done about it. Toward this end, I will bring two voices to set up some groundwork, two voices which may seem like an unusual pairing but nonetheless serve as guiding lights to the reader undergoing the path of inquiry Josh takes in this present work. We will start with the Aristotelian-Thomist philosopher Alasdair Macintyre, then turn to the chief theorist of the Situationist International,[1] cultural theorist Guy Debord.

In his classic work *After Virtue*,[2] Macintyre examines the moral disorder of the liberal, modern West. Macintyre traces

1 Formed in 1959, the SI was a collective of artists and social theorists that understood everyday life as enveloped within the capitalist mode of production and maintained by the power of the spectacle. To subvert the spectacle, the SI advocated creating "situations" (such as re-organizing city maps to intentionally get lost) that transform our relation to our environment from the mode of capitalist production to one of authentic encounter. While the group disbanded in 1972, it's influence is still felt today in projects such as random GPS.

2 MacIntyre Alasdair C. 2007. *After Virtue: A Study in Moral Theory* Third ed. Notre Dame Indiana: University of Notre Dame Press.

our modern moral malaise to the dream of the enlightenment philosophers: to arrive at consensus through the application of universal reason free from the perspectival prejudices of tradition. With the advent of the heralded objectivity of the natural sciences, the same pretension to objectivity would come to define the work of social scientists. With the discovery of the natural laws of the universe, the same operative reasoning would be applied to human societies and behavior; as humans are also natural, so too could behavior be understood with lawlike regularity. The work of the natural sciences would proceed through a non-teleological mechanistic metaphysics, forced to divulge its secrets through experimental manipulation, and ultimately arriving at how we can manipulate nature for our own ends. The same process culminating in the domination of non-human nature would come to be applied to human nature, with the rise of the cult of social-science informed experts and bureaucrats. The pretension to understand human nature through lawlike regularity would drive the role of government, institutions, and the workplace away from the teleological conception of the common good toward maximal efficiency of output while the moral flourishing of the citizenry would be delegated to the private life. The moral flourishing of the private life itself would become severely diminished, as the political sphere of consensus-making demanded the application of universal reason free from tradition. With rival traditions and religious commitments banished to the private sphere of individual opinion, the demand to adjudicate competing claims through a neutral universal language of reason privileged secularism and the concomitant encroachment of maximal production-oriented efficiency into all spheres of life. But at the same time and from the advent of enlightenment philosophy itself, skepticism entered onto the scene.

As the natural science of the enlightenment would upend man from a privileged position in the cosmos, the philosophy of the enlightenment would bring the center of reality to the individual itself. From Descartes' substance dualism to Kant's *a priori* categories in the *Critique of Pure Reason,* the subject-oriented foundationalism of modernism would yield to its irresolvable tension between the subject-constituted perception of the world and the world "out there". The line from skepticism seeded in modernist philosophy would come to fruition in the early 20th century with the still thoroughly modernist "masters of suspicion": Marx, Nietzsche, and Freud.[3] Moral theory would undergo a transformation, divorced from the both descriptive and prescriptive teleological conceptions of the common good, to an explanatory-psychologistic account of "emotivism".[4] The source of morality becomes understood as psychology, in the tastes and dispositions of the individual. With the moral commitments of traditions banished to the private sphere, they are no longer taken as simply no longer relevant to the public exercise of consensus-making but as an irrational impediment to a truly rational organization of the social sphere. Macintyre opts for the Aristotelian-Thomistic over the Nietzschean response to the crisis inaugurated in modernity but a full treatment of Macintyre's solution is

3 The name "masters of suspicion" was coined by the philosopher Paul Ricoeur. Ricoeur argued that Descartes instigated doubt but retained the coinciding of meaning with the certainty of consciousness. The masters of suspicion took it a step further so that the certainty of consciousness itself could no longer be maintained. For Nietzsche, our sense of the ethical is permeated by our physiological and emotive constitution. For Marx, the false consciousness of ideology is at the root of our conscious life. And for Freud, we are governed by latent unconscious drives. Therefore, these thinkers inaugurated suspicion right into the heart of human self-understanding.

4 In meta-ethics, non-cognitivism denotates the view that ethical sentences are not expressions of facts and do not contain truth values. Emotivism is one brand of non-cognitivism defended by philosophers such as Alfred Ayer. Ayer understands moral judgements as emotional expressions of approval or disapproval. According to Ayer, to exclaim "stealing is wrong!" expresses no proposition which could be true or false. Rather, it is a feeling that is being expressed.

not necessary here. What we look to in preparation for Josh's treatment of suspicion and the conspiracy theory lies in what Macintyre sees as moral *incommensurability.* Inspired by the philosophy of science found in the work of Thomas Kuhn,[5] Macintyre sees the cracking lines in the foundationalist Enlightenment project of universal reason through the impossibility of autonomous moral reasoning and the differing definitions of rationality itself. Simply put, moral pluralism of the type demanded in liberal democracy is impossible due to the irreducible and incompatible differences of conceptual foundations and traditions alike. It is not enough to say that dialogue among rival conceptions is difficult; debate over the public good is impossible when a commonly held basis of what the good is no longer exists. In agreement with the postmodernists, we assert that the rationalist planners, experts, bureaucrats, and media priests of liberal democracy are not laying claim to a truly universal reason but are merely one such tradition themselves. John Rawls be damned.

We now turn to our other figure before we meet them together and set the stage for Josh's work to follow. In his 1967 work *The Society of the Spectacle,* the critical theorist Guy Debord wrote a series of aphorisms to explore how our social life devolved into cultural homogenization, alienation from

5 Historian and Philosopher of Science Thomas Kuhn developed the idea of a paradigm in his account of scientific practice in his highly influential work The *Structure of Scientific Revolutions (Kuhn, T. (1970). The structure of Scientific Revolutions. Chicago University press).* In Kuhn's view, a scientific paradigm is a shared disciplinary matrix of theories, standards of measurement, metaphysical assumptions, instruments, and importantly, a shared set of problems that the scientific community in question works to solve. When there are competing paradigms (for example, Aristotelian vs. Newtonian paradigms) with a differing disciplinary matrix, adjudication between them is not possible. This is because each paradigm deals with different assumptions, a different standard of measurement, and a different set of problems. This is what is called incommensurability. Alasdair Macintyre applies this insight to worldviews and traditions as incommensurable moral paradigms.

the authentic lived experience of nature and community, the obfuscation of the past, and the intrusion of the commodity into all spheres of life. The concept Debord introduces, which serves as the focal point to describe the new set of mediated social practice, is named the Spectacle. To speak about the spectacle is not merely to speak about the dominance of mass media, of advertising, of the cult of celebrity, of social media, or any conglomeration of new media technologies. To limit our analysis of the spectacle to each of these media technologies would be to limit our analysis to the instruments of delivery. Rather, we must turn away from seeing the spectacle as a collection of images that exist as a sort of distraction to our social life, and instead come to understand the spectacle as the social relation itself mediated by images. Debord speaks of the history of consumption and more broadly, of social life itself, as having undergone a gradual decline from being, to having (in the manner of possession and consumption), and into merely appearing. The "merely appearing" denotes the transformation of possession of commodities into mere representation; as the colonization of the commodity has extended into social life itself, life becomes an accumulation of spectacles no longer directly lived.

Now it remains for us to draw out the power of the spectacle in our daily lives with a few direct examples. Through social media, the aspiration to achieve a globally connected community is given representation with the participation in trends among diverse populations. Difference is collapsed in a stream of images on Instagram and TikTok shorts, giving the appearance of universal sameness across time and cultures. The influencer celebrity makes his or her life into a commodity through carefully selected representation; while the average content consumer carefully mimics this activity of following the same trends, dubbing themselves the "protagonist". As new desires and social causes are created, followed, and enacted, the remaining bonds of friendship, affectivity, and opinions are collected to be monetized. Our natural affinities of family, friendship, and local community come to be infected with the newly constructed desires and social causes occurring with each new trend, to the point that those natural affinities themselves are effectively infected and severed. "*The closer their life comes to being their own creation, the more they are excluded from that life" (thesis 33).*[6] Ultimately, atomization is achieved through participation in the spectacle: separation perfected.

In another chapter of Debord's work, "Negation and Consumption within Culture", Debord describes the ways in which modern liberalism assures its legitimacy through the re-appropriation of older events, ideas and cultural arrangements. We can again adapt Debord's insights here to our own present situation with a few examples. This process serves a dual purpose and can be readily seen in popular television. In the first instance, it is to exploit the seductive intrigue of pre-modern political power. Simultaneously, an object of disgust and an object of fascination, the commodification of the past hierarchical Western arrangements into an often exaggerated or outright libelous portrayal serves as a justification for the Whig narrative of progress we inhabit today.[7] The other side of the process concerns the obfuscation of the past. As major

6 Guy Debord, *The Society of the Spectacle* (New York, Zone Books, revised edition, 1995), 24.

7 Whiggism refers to the principles and philosophy of the British Whig party. Originating as the parliamentarian faction in the Wars of the Three Kingdoms (1639 — 1651) and inspired by the political philosophy of John Locke, the Whig party advocated the supremacy of Parliament, toleration of dissenting Protestants, and opposition to a Catholic ascending to the Throne. In opposition to the Torys, the Whigs were the progressive party of revolution toward liberty and tolerance. The historian Herbert Butterfield coined the term "Whig history" as a critique of historiographical narratives of progress from out of a dark medieval Catholic past and toward the present Protestant and secular enlightenment of liberty and democracy. Butterfield argued that historians engaged in Whig history read the standards of the present back into the past, greatly distorting the nature of historical events, actors, and change.

historical figures and events are re-interpreted and re-written through racial and gender swapping, the sense of history is abolished. The past ceases to exist as it yields to the artificial characterization of the present, resulting in the present order's illusion of permanence. Even historical events and figures from as close as twenty years ago become reinterpreted from the appearance of the present in the new media. The disappearance of the past through the mode of its appearance in the present is not merely the abolishment of history; it is the abolishment of the future. As the sense of history is obliterated through repudiation and re-appropriation, the present gains an apparent permanency both in terms of preferential moral legitimacy and ontological immovability. The future, as a truly possible future and not merely the stretching forth repetition of the same present, never appears as an option in this condition. To paraphrase Slavoj Zizek, it is easier to imagine the end of the world than the end of the present order.

At last, we reach the point for Josh's work to meld these two separate strands of thinking with two separate concerns about liberalism together. We follow, with Macintyre, the affirmation that the process of consensus-building through the rationalist planning of bureaucrats and experts has failed. At the formation of America, Liberalism was an ideology that uprooted man from his organic identity—yet it was successfully implemented in a WASP population that was nonetheless rooted and homogenous. The European and Christian assumptions about the world and the moral order remained rooted in America and persisted with the arrival of other European ethnicities—certainly with their own organic differences and not without tension, but the shared European and Christian backgrounds allowed some degree of commensurability. As the ideology of universal sameness according to the norms of shared participation in reason reached its ultimate test with the arrival of non-European immigration with different histories and religious understanding and America's own gradual secularization among its founding stock, the project of consensus-building began to break down. The laws of human behavior could not be mapped like scientific laws and the demands of a shared ethics in the public space could not be reached without reference to one's prior and often tacit foundational commitment. The cult of the expert, therefore, began to break down. With the political campaign of Donald Trump, the mismanagement of Covid-19, the Epstein island revelations, and a seemingly never-ending stream of scandals involving the ruling class and its experts that still continues to this very moment of typing, the cracks present in the system's foundations and the mixture of malice with incompetence among elites was made apparent. The present order entered what Josh will call the "*permanent state of exception*". Now that liberal theory is itself exhausted, no longer able to neither account for or to navigate the crises of its own making, the liberal order turns from external triumphs to domestic scapegoats, seeking to define itself by its enemies rather than its results (to paraphrase Debord once again). The spectacle arrives with liberalism in its totalitarian phase, our combination of MacIntyre and Debord's descriptions now to be given a name, what Josh will call the *Neo-Real.*

We now come full circle, as the trafficking of suspicion and the conspiracy theory goes mainstream with the populist reaction to the mounting illegitimacy of the reigning political order and its cult of experts. Likewise, the experts themselves scramble to explain their declining acceptance and—without a hint of critical introspection—see the only possible answer to be a conspiracy of mastermind manipulators who direct a mob of irrational bigoted religious right-wingers against their own interests. Standing in the way of the authority of the expert is the conspiracy theorist, himself embroiled in a right-wing conspiracy to destroy the American way of freedom in favor of White supremacy and patriarchy. Such conspiracy theories find themselves repeated in the democratic panel of the debate stage and in the hysterics of liberal media without a hint of irony. Equally so, the conspiracy-minded right-populist sees the progressive left's hysterics as a project of control against the American way of freedom by global elites on the path to a world government. In both instances, each side claims to be defending the historic principles of the American way of life from the threat of tyranny, and both traffic in suspicion. The American populace, fully inhabiting the Neo-Real spectacle, is caught up in this ever-shifting storm of suspicion which threatens to overwhelm the weak foundation of the ship, split it in two, and sink all the passengers.

The stage is now set for Josh's work to follow. Having already analyzed the development of political extremism from the pathologies of liberal governance, he now turns our attention to what is an even more fundamental and generative pathology of the liberal worldview. In the course of carrying out his analysis, Josh brings forth two additional important insights alongside the whole of his argument concerning the phenomenology of conspiracy theories. The first insight is that liberalism, with its concomitant claim to the whole of reality and which has the appearance of permanence through the imposition of the Neo-Real, is a contingent force in history. The second insight follows from the first. As liberalism is a contingent force in history, its own history can be re-narrated as we seek to escape the bonds of cynical reason—in short, to not only redeem our past but to envision a true future negating the corrosive expansion of the "open society". Josh continues his perceptive analysis of pathologies underlying liberal progress begun in *American Extremist,* now unearthing the trafficking of suspicion endemic to everyday discourse in America; the destructive consequences of liberal success resulting in violence that is very real. Unlike the catastrophic violence of the American Empire's past interventions into foreign countries, as it is a domestic bubbling of everyday conflict, it can no longer be ignored or kept at a distance as entertainment on the television screen. Each side of suspicion is manifested in end-of-the-world hysterics at the holiday family reunion. The "experts" of social science truly concerned with achieving peaceful consensus and disturbed at the crisis of increasing moral/political incommensurability would do well to heed Josh's analysis and prescription.

Tyler Hamilton
September 2023

UNDERSTANDING CONSPIRACY THEORIES

CHAPTER ONE

The Existential and Political Crisis of Trustlessness

Our time may be characterized strongly, if not entirely, by disunity, disagreement, and discontinuity, and yet we all acknowledge the following truth: we are living through an extended and unprecedented crisis—a series of crises, even, given familiarity (and, as a result, rendered mundane) by the uniformity and ubiquity of liberal democratic institutions. Somehow this compounded banality only intensifies these crises, tipping us into a nigh terminal condition of apoplectic helplessness.

Do we dare probe this temperamental consensus further? If asked to identify (in as much detail as one can summon) the precise nature of the challenges confronting us, our stormy consonance dissipates once more. "*What is going on?*" "*Who is behind it?*" "*What do they seek?*" Suddenly a plethora of antagonists and plots emerge, some more plausible than others, and each one more nefarious and apocalyptic than the next. What we are left with more closely resembles a grocery list than it does a line-up of would-be perpetrators. But the meaning behind this cataclysmic tumultuousness is more profound than the simple fact that people no longer agree on basic facts and principles, or that they no longer care to "get along" with one another. *Misinformation. Disinformation. Extremism. Fanaticism.* (The four horsemen of the neoliberal apocalypse.) No, things are far graver than that. We are incapable of coming to agreement because we have been rendered incapable of trust. It is not merely that we do not know *who* or *what* to trust, but that we no longer know *how* to trust. Even irony, the presumed nadir of civilizational affect local to the waning years of the 20th century, for all its skepticism of authority and its ode to non-enjoyment, still believed in a counter-culture—still held articles of faith. It still permitted itself a sliver of (highly qualified) enjoyment, a sliver which has since given way to the complete disavowal of joy (and along with it: faith and trust). We will turn our attention to the problem of joylessness later. For now, trustlessness remains our object of inquisition.

The trust faculty, shall we call it, having been slowly whittled to a nub—or better still, eroded like the face of the Sphinx by wave after unending wave of political force—points to nowhere and everywhere all at once, leaving the individual and his community with only their confused instinct and their degenerate conditioning to guide them. That instinct, man's capacity for deep learning (honed long before ever drawing his first breath), finds itself immersed in a foreign space—a construction only superficially like the space which birthed it; except that to describe it as "superficial" is not truly accurate. Rather, we ought to speak of the *artificial* as opposed to the *superficial*, for this foreign space is in fact a simulacrum of the originary order which has informed man's conduct since time immemorial (that is to say, *the order of a given tradition*).

To better understand this problem of trustlessness we ought to designate a name for the space to which embodied instinct is now bound. For now, we may term it *neo-Reality*, *neo-Realism*, or *the neo-Real* (*nR*, henceforth), with "neo" indicating a repetition of as well as, in some meaningful sense, a departure from some "Real", itself defined as a primary (or privileged) space of processes, techniques, and methods necessary for producing sociality. The *nR* is purely a political construction (with mass media, the courts, and the various other managerial institutions and networks serving as its midwives); *nR* is "real" (or actual, can be said to exist) insofar as it descends from an authentic and spontaneous originary Real and purports to "carry the torch" of the Real. By proposing this concept, we are assuming a territory or state which has descended into intrigue and turmoil, either resulting from internal factors (conventional intrapolitical conflict, such as between rival institutions or factions), the introduction of some foreign element (sociobiological conflict), or a combination of the two. The quest to establish *nR* is synonymous with the desire to establish a new regime, or hegemonic system of control.

Behind the prefix is another altogether different suggestion, however, enjoining us to understand *nR* not solely as a "new" construct, but also as a "reduction from" and a "distillation of" (to be elaborated more fully in the following paragraphs) that originary Real. From the point of view of the (new, emerging) state, it is a positive, spontaneous—and necessary—break, an innovation upon that which preceded. Simultaneously it purports to be an act of political revival, bringing something back which was lost while all the while modifying it to fit contemporary, pragmatic ends. Disruptions in the implementation of this new mode of life (such as emergent contradictions, deliberate falsehoods, hypocrisies) are ameliorated through the power of the dominant institutions (aided, when necessary, by the direct application of state power), thus ensuring that *nR* is made non-usurpable by the governed. A rather textbook historical example of *nR* would be the open society of liberal philosopher, Karl Popper, though it will take us some time before we are able to further draw out the specificities of this example (we shall investigate this more deeply in the third chapter). The Straussian legacy of finding democratic pluralist priors strewn across history is another such example, though we shall not investigate that fact any further here. With a view of *nR* in mind, one might find any number of examples merely by reviewing the literature produced in our present so-called postwar order.

Turning away from the impartial description of the phenomenon in favor of a view from the point of critique, we should take the meaning of "neo" to be a deliberate and pre-meditated casting away of, or unshackling from, a state of containment and deprivation, and thus away from a "Real" condition of "horror" (e.g., upheaval, persecution, or discrimination) the likes of which those who had endured it would never seek a return. Prepending on a common noun in this way carries, in my view, a heavy and ominous connotation, as it so often seems to smuggle alongside it the introduction of something distasteful if not altogether intolerable. Whether one thinks of neo-Darwinist science, neo-Soul music, or neo-Classical architecture, it is always plainly obvious that he is confronted with a simulacrum—and, furthermore, a rather sinister one at that. *nR* is a simulation of reality and of the law in just the same way as neo-Darwinism is a simulation of the scientific theory of evolution, or how the music of John Legend or Amy Winehouse are mere simulacra of Motown compositions and not, themselves, genuine works of original harmonic construction.

However, it is not only that they are merely representations of familiar things which should trouble us, but also that they are representations delivered to us by influential members of a detached and hostile regime. Distorted by the particularistic intentions of the men and women perpetrating these repetitions, what comes back to us is not only *different* from what it once was but also *lesser* than it was. Whether cynical or earnest, done with an eye toward commodity value or social value, desirable or undesirable in its outcome, what we receive is never *in its essence* identical to its ancestor, neither in presentation nor effect. Not only does it fail to be a faithful representation, but in fact we often find quite important details left out. (There is a suspicious remainder which jeopardizes the entire project, for the project is in some way predicated on the dismissal of this suspicion-worthy excess). That which such recapitulations present as new and different often carry a reactionary (in the pejorative sense), defensive, and otherwise ego-chauvinistic quality which stymies the extraction of some social or moral value. More succinctly, they are a malicious appropriation. Via this appropriation, *nR* enables (or is synonymous with) the imposition of a mode or habit of sociality which militates against the order of Reality which organically constitutes a given territory or state. Not all cultures or civilizations traffic in the production of *nR*, as commonly seen throughout history when people-groups were simply destroyed or replaced as opposed to maintained in a semi-hypnotic state (as is the case with *nR*). Stability (of a kind) is therefore implied by *nR*, giving us some insight into the reasoning behind its implementation. The more legitimate (in the sense of serving a broad eusocial aim) the form *nR* takes, the medium of professional sports for example, the more intrinsically stable *nR* is, as the emotional energies provoked by the system are easily managed. Less legitimate forms, for instance State ideologies like multiculturalism, come with an expiration date for the foundational social forces themselves are too volatile. As for the specific ways in which a given order of *nR* asserts itself or comes to be, the precise circumstances are themselves highly contingent. *How* it arises is less a question of theoretical principle and more of biographical happenstance. We concern ourselves more with the *fact* of its emergence, and that wherever it does emerge, we observe a necessary (and quantifiable) decline in social trust. In due time we will explain the conditions which give rise to the *nR* but for now, we must delve deeper into the relationship between *nR* and the Real. While the *nR* is a simulacrum it is also a supersession, a kind of colonizing or reterritorializing of the Real (that is, of an organically occurring and primordial sociality) such that we can no longer hold a concept of the organic Real without subjecting it first to ideology (cynicism) or naivete. Presently, our distorted view of pre-sexual revolution domestic politics serves as an instructive example of this: questions of domesticity, sexual ethics, and all related intersexual dynamics rarely escape the clutches of hypermodern suspicion (e.g., fourth-wave feminism, men's rights activism, et cetera); instead they are exorcised of their contingency and made compatible with the presentism of *nR*.

In short, suspicion of the primary and the primordial becomes a fundamental and unquestionable social affect, intrapsychically bolstering the new regime. Through juridical power, *nR* makes the Real other; led by a procession of legalists, the whole of society is dragged into an entirely new mode, a new ontology, of life. Pedantry increasingly becomes an accompanying feature of all disciplines and domains of life, as not only do legalists take the reins of society but we all, in our hearts, become little legalists, too. The further the *nR* ascends above the Real, the deeper into its shadow the Real descends and thus the more laborious a reversal then becomes. We should note, of course, that to speak of a triumph of the *nR* over the Real is just another way to speak of the "ascension or coronation of the order of *a specific type of man* over that which had only just prevailed", and so naturally the triumph of the *nR* is simply a polite way to describe the blinding of an indigenous or primordial man by some outside force via a particular and exacting application of the law. Implicit to this analysis is an assumption of indirect hostility, by which I denote a *meaningful-but-non-violent force* that has been applied *in concert* against some population. (That legal strategies of force can be, and often are, supplemented, where necessary, by formal and traditional demonstrations of force is a fact which does not by itself invalidate or weaken the theory being proposed.)

And so, man's instinct—while not exactly useless—is hardly the magic bullet some would make it seem. Rehabilitation is, of course, possible; subjecting oneself to the cleansing fire of an intentional ascetic practice (supported by one's tribe) can undo the psychopolitical consequences of juridical-cultural warfare. Lacking the social infrastructure necessary for such a restoration, the vulgar hybrid of Pavlovian-Skinnerian thought which directs much of the social order (demonstrating the frightening potency of 20th century psychology, though not necessarily its veracity or depth) stymies the exorcism of false consciousness, tragically manipulating Man's confused instincts. So effective is this hybridized psychological program that even when man feels he is acting in a noble or fruitful manner, his conduct may still further the ends of his marionettist. He may still succeed (and depending on his nature likely will); however, his accomplishments will always and forever be on some other man's terms, which is to say, within the imagination of an alien. He or she will know some approximation of love, joy, and fulfillment, but in the end their choices will ultimately and unknowingly undermine the genuine striving for happiness, duty, and honor.

For societies which make the vivisection and analysis of Man a top priority, the fact of man's present trustlessness poses a far more fatal threat. It would already be calamitous enough if, for example, the informational ecosystem was merely contaminated, infiltrated, or otherwise gamed in some way which impaired its constituent members (gravely or otherwise); were we merely confronted with some discrete locality of adversariality, perversion, or vice, this alone would pose a serious enough challenge. Sadly, circumstances are far more troubling than this. It is not merely a question of "contamination" or "gamification", for the well has been poisoned and the people doing the poisoning are studying its effects on the well-drinkers to better innovate superior methods of well-poisoning. Observations made of each well-drinker and his or her unique interaction are taken and measured against the whole, with the most promising results extracted, refined, and then reintroduced as a formal technique: a permanent and perfectly quantifiable feedback loop for the cultivation and implementation of knowledge-power.

As for the modalities of implementation, we may think of this program in terms of being either…

1. Implemented, should one prefer to think linearly and arborescently, downwardly in uniform manner (carrying the assumption of unity, cohesion, and most significantly—intentionality), or
2. Implanted, were we to think in terms of centrality—and the human body even—with suspicion radiating and rippling out across the whole body (whether we think of a body of water, a body politic, or once more, a human body) from the very center of influence to its outermost limits,[1] or as
3. Emergent, as in a form of semi-stochastic and rhizomorphic movement, emphasizing spontaneity, creativity, and freedom.[2] All three are correct, as far as they each describe either a phase within or a style of disruptive political programming. Different poisons work in different ways, and more importantly, those who do the poisoning have different methods and approaches at their disposal depending on the characteristics immanent to their tribe or circumstance. Deliber-

1 Here, the assumption remains of a kind of uniformity and logic. However, we are not speaking of the uniformity or logic of rational, philosophic Man but of the uniformity/logic usually counterposed by artists, poets, and scientists. It has a logic and a direction, and we may come to discover it, but it remains distal. I would say as well that "implantation" must be thought of as a covert, hidden maneuver, and as a kind of subterfuge. After all, where else may something be implanted but "within"? This distinguishes "implantation" from "implementation", for innate to the implementation of a program is the presence and identifiability of those doing the implementation. Implantation is faceless whereas implementation has a face (often a multiplicity of faces).

2 Emergent programs have a unity to them as well; however, it is not the unity of the implemented program, which binds through domineering martial values, but rather the unity of egoists (in the Stirner-ite sense) or free souls (in the Nietzschean sense).

> ation over the precise form of its delivery abound, for that is the nature of man, but there can be no doubt as to the fact of the poison's presence or its insidious effects on contemporary American society.

Suspicion has become second nature for us—*and justifiably so!* Americans (as is also the case for Canadians, Australians, and Europeans) have stood by and borne the brunt of violent consequences wrought by the alien rivalries which have exploded across their homelands. Most recently, they have endured forced austerity imposed by their leaders' support for the Russia-Ukraine war, a barely restrained domestic race war (in the form of the George Floyd riots), and the decimation of their economies *and* critical institutions caused by the same leaders' mismanagement of COVID-19, and all in the span of only a few years. And while the primacy of doubt is evident merely by pointing to the very recent past, its origins do not lie in sight of our historical rearview mirror. Later in this work I will demonstrate the longer, more complex history of suspicion (more commonly discussed in spookier, more pejorative terms, like *conspiratorialism*), highlighting those critical points which accelerated us into the presently intolerable circumstance.

The massive transparency society of global technocracy has democratized suspicion and curiosity (the karmic boomerang of a society operating on an axiomatic open-mindedness) such that the ever-metastasizing surveillance state no longer operates unidirectionally. *We*, as it turns out, are the ones who watch the watchers. As a result, theories of shadowy conspirators with Machiavellian schemes are now the norm because (to anyone with the eyes to see) collusion itself is an open fact. No one doubts the reality of collusion just as we no longer doubt the existence of Evil. In the case of both collusion and Evil, the only worthwhile remaining debate is about their respective *depths*.

Although it is the duplicity, the self-servingness, and the complicity in Evil of our leaders which has thrust us into this crisis of suspicion, nonetheless the proliferation of "the conspiracy theory" is as much a problem for *us* as people who must live, and toil, and seek fulfillment in the bombed-out warzone known as the hypermodern West, as it is for those who rule us. As I have said, it is the third chapter wherein I will discuss the historical antecedents to our present moment, providing us with a more complete understanding as to why *our* experience of suspicion is so *uniquely* perilous. Pending that exploration, the fact remains as such: we no longer need to endure generations, or simple lifetimes even, to witness the collapse of an idea as lived through the people it has taken residence within. Under hypermodernity, we can observe the consequences of epistemic crisis within a matter of years. Depending on the nature of the crisis, this may happen perhaps within a period of only a few months. In some cases, it may occur for the simple reason of an individual or community naively persisting within their paradigm, previously impervious to certain modifications within the program, for whom the sudden and inconceivable confrontation with *nR* results in instant annihilation (e.g., previously well-guarded identity-groups now overtaken by fresher progressive tides). Hypermodernity, though, offers an impossibly and perplexingly vast array of outcomes, not all of them bad ones.[3] Only just recently, on the eve of a momentous surge in her career, a sitting U.S. congresswoman claimed that her flirtation with the radical wing of her party was merely the result of what we shall term an *'involuntary immersion'* into the hyperworld of politics.[4]

3 With the procession of the hypermodern epoch fully under way, one gets the impression that a central tenet of hypermodernity is that you can get absolutely anything and everything except for what you want.

4 Vlamis, Kelsey, n.d. "Rep. Marjorie Taylor Greene Said 'like a Lot of People' She Had 'Easily Gotten Sucked into Some Things I Had Seen on the Internet' Regarding QAnon Conspiracy Theories". Business Insider. https://www.businessinsider.com/marjorie-taylor-greene-got-sucked-in-

Anything (and, paradoxically, nothing at all) is possible within hypermodern America.

In the coming chapters we will explore the phenomenology of conspiratorialism, the nature of the conspiracy theorist, and much more. But for now, we must turn our attention to a yet unexplored factor in the production of suspicion.

A Permanent State of Exception

Having come to a common understanding of *nR*, we now arrive at the critical question: what are the political conditions which give rise to the *nR* and its culture of suspicion? Already we have given some indications. Now, let us proceed even further.

In the United States, at least, the crisis of trustlessness began in earnest sometime after it achieved the position of global hegemon, thereby claiming the seat of the throne of a worldwide empire. Certainly, America's presence on the world stage was perceptible long before the dawning of the 21st century, that stature germinating new and uneasy tensions at home. With a broader view in mind, it could be easily argued that certain definitive moments of the preceding century were in fact responsible for seeding the sentiments and potentialities which we are only now developing a language for. Those arguing as such may well be correct. (Our analysis will, in time, include some of those very instances, for example, concerns over communist infiltration into the dominant sectors of American life.) More astute observers of history may no doubt locate more exacting moments far earlier in the nation's history which could have the effect of complicating or deepening these theoretical workings. Doubt is every bit a challenge to politics as it is to epistemology. But each epoch of American history cultivated its own culture of suspicion, contingent on

to-qanon-conspiracy-theories-internet-2023-1 (accessed December 07, 2023).

the circumstances of the time. At present, however, this reliable production of suspicion accumulates, metastasizes, and threatens to overtake us. While we are the inheritors of a great American tradition of doubt, there is indeed something peculiar about this specific time.

Summarizing the centuries-long history of a nation and its peoples is a difficult and doubtless foolish thing to do; however, there is one thing that likely could not be said about any prior period in American history: from the time of the Soviet Union's collapse onward, the United States of America had entered a completely novel period in its history. A peerless time without enemies. Concrete enemies, that is: ones with flags and charters, national anthems and beauty pageants. How, when every nation-state of consequence has been grafted to America's global economic network (thus made docile, dominable, and compliant), could it possibly have any *real* enemies? When everyone is forced to speak America's language, barter in her currency, and entertain themselves with her dreams and aspirations, and when the absolute difference between America and its peers vanishes (in conceptual terms but increasingly in material terms as well), how can it be said to have enemies? As both a matter of national security and individual patriotic sentiment, such a thing would cease to be possible.

Great masses of men (e.g., the nation-state and the imperial state), know the ailments and vices which befall us as individuals every bit as well as we do and as such, upon securing a hard-fought victory, the United States settled into a period of restlessness. And whenever the door is opened to restlessness, internal division is sure to scurry in and establish a camp inside one's home. Such was the case when concerns over external, so-called fundamentalist Islamic terrorism (a new kind of "enemy") slowly morphed into concerns about homegrown "White Supremacist" terror cells. During the time in which this transition occurred (less than twenty years), the hysteria and bloodlust manifested in support of America's latest foe (itself) was so totalizing and complete that the country managed to lose its patience for one of its favorite pastimes: enthusiasm for liberal dustups with abstract spooks ("The War on Christmas", "The War on Drugs", etc.) waned and all warfare—symbolic or otherwise—targeted the domestic population (with its White population receiving the most sustained and vicious punishment imaginable).

The United States had entered the totalitarian phase of its imperial career, and with it as well, into *a permanent state of exception.* It is important to note that a state moves into totalitarianism once it has exhausted the limits of its political theory and no longer possesses the creative freedom to navigate exceptional instances of history. This is not to confuse all direct applications of state power with totalitarianism (a very liberal thing to do, I might add); rather, it is to acknowledge the state's tendency toward brutality once it permits itself to ignore crucial political realities. Resultantly, the political body must be moved into a permanent state of exception (*PSoE* henceforth) to obscure the fact of its negligence, but also to deny the emergence of a truly sovereign political entity—one which would rival and overthrow the existing regime. In one fell swoop, the state forecloses not only the possibility of genuine and righteous authority, but also, the possibility of justice as well. This changing of direction, or said better, the introduction of a new civilizational telos (exemplified as it is by our present shift into totalitarian imperialism) drives domestic alienation as much as any economic or technological pressure, casting ever more members of society into some condition of dissidence (whether they realize it or not).[5] In short, the *PSoE*

5 Often, they do not (that is, until the baton—metaphorical or otherwise—cracks them in the back of the head). In many ways this is far more sinister than anything concocted by the Soviet regime. Technocratic global neoliberalism has made implicit and occluded that which the Soviet states could achieve through no other way but brute force. We can attribute this to the characterological differences innate to the respective people-groups in leadership, but also to changing attitudes in governmentality resulting

is a sinister solution to the problems associated with managing a precarious domestic population during a period of intensifying expansion, complexity, and peerlessness.

But the *PSoE* is more than just a suspension of the reigning legal and social norms: it is also an ontological suspension of reality itself. Contained within the *PSoE* is the whole of a territory's political and existential life, flattened, recombined, inflated, or neglected in whatever ways deemed necessary for the success and furtherance of the new state (in the case of the contemporary United States, the totalitarian imperial state—*TIS* henceforth). The state of exception (*SoE*) denotes a culmination or expression of a pure power, a pure political act and a capacity for action, one that operates to secure itself in a climate of tremendous uncertainty by transcending or superseding the law and thus ascending, temporarily, to the plain of *aperioristos* (limitlessness, a condition of being absolute) in a fatal but necessary act of creative destruction. The *PSoE*, on the other hand, is indicative of an absolute despotism or totalitarianism, as we have said, and in a profound sense represents an inversion and a degradation of the original Schmittian conception.

The *SoE* is a decisive moment of choosing, wherein the authority to "realize" and "resolve" a crisis through apperception and will are discovered (or declared) via the sovereign's action. In the case of the *PSoE*, however, all has been prearranged and preordained. There is neither decisiveness nor spontaneity, rather, there is merely implementation of the predetermined. Within the *PSoE*, true sovereignty does not exist (true in the sense of a sovereign acting as a genuine representative of the governed). Actually-existing-sovereignty occurs elsewhere, obscured, while on the domestic plain *visible sovereignty* and the political process of sovereignty carry all the gravitas and significance of a game of charade. Given its fundamentally duplicitous conceit, the *PSoE* is a rule by super-sovereigns

from the ascendancy of neoliberalism.

whereas only the *SoE* may reveal authentic (or folk) sovereignty. "Sovereignty" within the *PSoE* is only about the authority to obfuscate, to ambiguate, and to "act" (in the sense of theatricality, not in the sense of forward-directedness, or as in an act of political consequence) out a series of justifications, appeals, and rationalizations which provide the necessary churn for the manufacturing of consent within the *TIS*. This authority, however, is always "under direction"; it is a delegative or extended authority and not a creative or true authority. (It is an authority in the same way that the thug who breaks your legs on the orders of his boss is "an authority".) Let me reiterate: the instantiation of the *PSoE* precedes the permanent deterioration in a regime's legitimacy. But it also accompanies this deterioration, therefore sharing in the same farcical absurdity. *TIS* can only stand tall so long as it can stand at all, and ours will not enjoy genuine and unquestioned moral supremacy before it collapses under the weight of its own excess. (The United States, while no longer plausible as a heroic exemplar of world governance, nonetheless enjoys a sliver of moral supremacy thanks to its successful strategy of juvenilizing all possible moral discourse at the geopolitical level. Through mimesis, theoretically rival states participate in international discourse using the linguistic conventions and cultural concepts invented by Western *TIS*, thereby extending its legitimacy, its expiry, further into time. People may not remember the details of the conflict, but they will remember on whose terms the conflict was dictated.)

Inflation of all things, a necessarily coextensive process along the way into the imperial phase of a people-group's development (which, incidentally, is the final phase of their development, at least in political terms), begins first as an inflation of the ego-ideal of the regime itself, and ends with the inflation of the average person's skeptical faculty, thereby obliterating his capacity for rational thought. A kind of inflated version of concept creep facilitates this *PSoE*, for in any totalitarian system, signs and their referents must continually expand or else the system will not have the room necessary to absorb (and reterritorialize) the whole of life's facticity. Conceptual creep as conventionally understood, describes the phenomenon by which concepts expand and conglomerate until the original meaning includes those things which do not strictly cohere. In truth, the semantic crisis is more profound and tragic than what I have just described; concepts are not merely hyperinflated, they are hyperactive—constantly in motion like a game of musical chairs, rearranging themselves to the detriment of executive level cognizing. I will speak more on this in the closing chapter, but suffice to say, the *PSoE* does not thrive merely by controlling thought, but also by negating it.

Related, though not identically so: concepts like that of "liberty" and "freedom" and "security" cannot be said to have the same meaning for those using them in the 19th century as they do for us, here, in the 21st. This semantical bloat seems to allow a given concept to absorb even its own negation, binding to the very notion itself (a dialectic which serves to frustrate simple conversation). For instance, we may take note of the fact that a formerly well-comprehended concept like "free speech", previously understood to mean the political protection to issue controversial statements, now contains within it its dialectical negation ("hate speech", controversial statements paradoxically determined to be exempt from political protection) such that even advocates of "free speech" must now answer for this paralogical extension into the conceptual (which, over time, necessarily becomes an extension into the actual). Conceptual and discursive maneuvers (really, retreats) such as these are increasingly reflected within our legal framework; the state will proceed with the new conceptualization, all while leaving the governed to apoplectically debate its content. All politics is psychopolitics, and so war waged upon Man's conceptual prowess takes many forms and occurs along multiple fronts. It is simple (and sufficient) enough to note currently that we are describing a process of complete and total discursive monopolization, such that all words and concepts mean whatever they need to mean at the precise moment the *TIS* needs them to change.

I use the term *PSoE* to highlight the political tendency to seize upon authentic folk sovereignty and constrain it, to wrest political power away from it, and to change the conditions under which sovereignty operates. Extra-legality, in effect, becomes the new judicial norm. After all, one must always stay at least one step ahead of his enemies. *nR* is therefore the content to the *PSoE*'s form; upon declaring an ongoing crisis, new norms are implemented which fundamentally alter the individual's direct experience of him or herself, as well as the world in which they live. Within the context of *nR*, alienation, estrangement, and anomie ought to be understood as expressions of political derealization (not to be understood in pathological terms, rather, but as the individual's first steps into a space of genuine living, free—though not at peace—from the tyrannical overcoding induced by the new supersovereign).

Governance Anxiety

The near *PSoE*, operating continuously, as we have said, for several decades (a conservative estimate but not meritless as a starting point for our discussion) could be interpreted as an anxiety *around governance itself* every bit as much as it could be understood as the fatal unfurling of a particular expression(s) of logic. In fact, the two may be intertwined with one another, were we to accept that *the atrocity of power itself* often compels leadership to choose decidedly fatalistic and mistakenly self-serving (or perhaps, self-preserving) courses of action.[6] To articulate the point more clearly: the absence of

6 For us to continue in any sensible manner, it is necessary for us to arrive at a useful (that is, *strict*) definition of power, at least one that suffices for our contemporary time. Power is the audacious performance of some role or deliverance of an act necessary to assure some desired end, be it object

confidence—or, even, the presence of too much confidence—among the ruling elites (as regards the mounting tensions within the global technocratic order, spurred by the rapid degree of technological and moral change) may cause them to err in some specifically non-ideological way, overcommit to poor strategies and methodologies, or, as I have suggested, it may be that the fumbling itself is a consequence of the pressures of having to be the one who chooses. And *that*, were we to be honest with ourselves we would readily admit, might be the most human folly of all, hardly worthy of the "conspiracizing" which is the ultimate target of this analysis. We see quite easily how the present epidemic of suspicion problematizes attempts by the average person to develop normative models of authority. Suspicion, conspiratorialism, whatever we wish to call it, often derives from the utter unintelligibility of sovereign power on the part of those who do not partake of it.

It would be fruitful, then, to discuss this atrocity further in hopes that we might deflate the paranoid neuroticism of contemporary suspicion-culture,[7] even if only modestly so. This atrocity of power (instantiated as it is by the following trifecta: the self-recognition of man's inappropriateness as ruler, the absolute necessity of man regardless of his inappropriateness, and the sublimity of Being and the challenges it poses to us) dialectically terrorizes Man, forcing him into error.[8] Whether we speak of life or death, the young or the old, the rich or the poor, liberty or security, progress or tradition, or any of the other existential tensions beset upon us, Man himself is the

or event. Definitionally—as well as affectively—power is about that which none would truly want, and moreover, that most could never possibly secure. Power is that which lies beyond mere desire.

7 "Suspicion-culture" should be understood as the sum of a social order's capacity to produce and direct doubt.

8 The trifecta may be stated more succinctly in the following way: Man understands the exclusionary reality of his own personal weakness, and yet he also recognizes that his vice is not, in fact, a disqualifying determinant in the face of God or history.

inflection point through which all things emerge. Governance, being a simulacrum of Godliness, poses all manner of conundrums and dilemmas to mankind. As such, man finds himself unfit for this station yet cannot abscond from his duty (hence his anxiety). Ideology, then, might have the characteristic of a coping mechanism designed to aid members of leadership in executing their duty. Ultimately, however, no ideology or coping strategy can permanently forestall a given society's conclusion or fulfillment. History (our very own recent history, no less!), indicates to us this fact: our own leaders, seeing themselves fit to judge the whole of man, commit themselves now to facilitating the descent of our civilization, and they have devised just the ideology for putting our way of life to rest. Finality, whether wrought nobly through conquest or natural cause – or pathologically viz. despair or obeisance – is still finality all the same. This too feeds sovereignty's nervousness.

The implicit *fact* of governance, particularly of a global technocratic governance operating (theoretically, at least) outside of traditional constraints and pressures thus "afforded" the challenges befitting a God (for instance, the power of life over death and the power of an absolute clairvoyance, one capable of banishing entropy and uncertainty), is rarely appreciated in and of itself. After all, nobody truly loves greatness so long as they stand apart from and outside of it. Whether it is true or not (and in our current state, the following statement could hardly be further from truth), leadership, authority, sovereignty, etc., are synonymous with "greatness". Excellence and virtuosity are bound up with the imaginal notion of greatness, and given the American prejudice for meritocratic organization, the association is only compounded further. For Americans, this association has become inescapable (as have its consequences). Tragically, our contemporary mode of living is predicated on the continued *unweaving* of society, such that whole stratums of society never make contact—the necessary consequence of which is the production of an infinitely mineable and societal wide epidemic of *ressentiment*. We become inaccessible to one another, not even capable of puncturing through this divide with the power of our imagination. Reverence for—or even mere begrudging acceptance of—greatness has become a lost art. While hatred and envy are virtually all that remain, it may still be possible to understand the nature of rulership without enabling such an emotionally charged perception of the matter.

Bearing this in mind, it must be said: one ought to feel one's very nerve-endings quiver in terror over the prospect of such a thing even existing (that "*thing*", of course, being our planetary civilization of billions, held together by electric light, existing in a state of nigh absolute imperturbability), let alone conceiving of—and grasping—the power which is required to rule it. The very possibility of such a power is stupefying in its awesomeness. Perhaps, then, it is this very stupefaction—and the complete and moral paralysis which follows in its wake—that we ought to direct our attention toward. For, we may locate within this stupefaction, this paralysis, a complete suspension of personhood (a form which only occurs when man attempts self-transcendence, the vain pursuit of singularity with God which incinerates both himself and, inevitably, his social order).

We may look to the Greek canon for historical analogues to this tendency we observe in our own time, specifically to the *Metamorphoses* and the story of Daedalus and Icarus—a story, from a certain point of view, about the causes and the processes of generational decline. Egotistical and inexperienced youth, both impetuous and libidinally excited, drives the competent but sentimental elder to pity; perhaps motivated by guilt (were we to imagine ourselves in such a circumstance, we, at least, might find ourselves feeling that way), Daedalus endeavors to deliver the two of them from imprisonment (a consequence of his own actions, and therefore a plausible cause for guilt-influenced misjudgment), utilizing his skill as a craftsman to do so. As they prepare to set out, freedom just over the horizon, Daedalus instructs Icarus on the use of his freshly designed wings. Youth rides high on the accomplishments of its forebears; upon striking out on their own they so often fall to their deaths, failing as Icarus did, to heed the sound words of their fathers. At least on this occasion, vigor be a vice.

The tale of the death of Icarus warns us not only of imprudence, but on the other hand of complacency, that countervailing force in our Grecian parallel. We seem to be obviously discussing the will, willfulness, striving, and all such related concepts—what room is there in all of this for complacency? Perhaps it was the complacency (expressed in the first lines of the poem) of Daedalus which intergenerationally, enantiodromiatically, drove Icarus toward his Faustian end.[9][10] If we are free to analyze (which we are) why would we assume the moral core of this story would only be true at the level of the individual, of the single-family unit, and that its deep wisdom wouldn't in fact compound at higher levels of social organization? Or, at an absolute minimum, that the accumulation of power over time within a single civilizational stratum would not affect debilitating consequences on the broader governmental ecosystem? A thorough recollection of the tale will demonstrate that technological power was very much an intergenerational affair for Daedalus, and that his inheritance granted him tremendous influence, wealth, and by one account, made him an object of worship. Further support of his strong lineage comes to us from *Apollodorus* (albeit in rather grim fashion), wherein Daedalus murdered his nephew Talos upon discovering that the boys' talent for craftwork rivaled his own.[11] Taken as a

9 Ovid, *Metamorphoses,* (Oxford University Press, 1970) Book XIII:
"In tedious exile now too long detain'd,
Daedalus languish'd for his native land."

10 Carl Jung uses the word "enantiodromia" to denote the psychological transformation of one affect, condition, or state, into its opposite.

11 *Apollodorus*, Library, Sir James George Frazer ed., book 3, chapter 15,

whole, the tragedy of Icarus' death is only an expression of a greater tragedy: his family's prowess, a world-historical prowess at that, thrashed within a single generation. Our Icarian parallel is not complicated by these observations so much as it is deepened: the complacency of elders and the restless vigor of youths are challenges to governance, but so too are envy and fear.[12] If anything, the story of Daedalus and Icarus serves as an insight into the phenomenology of power but also as a form of received wisdom, instructing us (if only negatively) on the multigenerational (mis)management of greatness. Daedalus knew all too well the atrocity of power (*AoP*, henceforth), for he lived it in his own life. Fortunately for the men and women of his time, Daedalus' death did not portend the collapse of their way of life. We, as hypermodern Americans (and Westerners) are under no such assurance, however, that present day leadership's failure to answer the *AoP* will not, in fact, throttle our very existence.

The power of life over death, and of technological mastery over the natural world, are conjoined with the terrible knowledge of their consequences. Only a rightful authority can grasp the magnitude of this fact; only a righteous authority couldunderstand the imperfection of the world and the fragility imposed by it upon those courageous enough to act upon it. To speak of governance anxiety within the context of the present epidemic of conspiratorial ideation is to reintroduce into the minds of skeptics the practical concerns associated with political action, with governance itself, and to extirpate the naïve Manichaeism which reduces history to the level of

section 8.

12 So great was Daedalus' pride for his talents, he became a victim of his own invention—ultimately being trapped within the labyrinth he had devised as punishment for conspiring against King Minos. This also strikes us as instructive, for we should all beware the dangers of being trapped by our own ambitions. (Particularly in our day, the notion of being unable to navigate the complex structures we have imposed upon ourselves seems especially apt.)

a melodramatic space opera[13]. For if conspiratorialism is ultimately about justice—that is, uncovering the truly malicious actors and disciplining them—then hysteria and stereotyping are of no use to us. I am not arguing sympathy for the devil, rather I am stating that if it were possible to imagine a just authority at all, we could still not possibly imagine the routine and incontrovertible weight such an authority necessarily bears as an executioner of sovereign power. That is, we certainly could not do so in the current unwoven condition of American society. But perhaps we could begin to imagine such a condition if we could begin to understand the true nature of power (as wielded by a genuine authority). We will attempt such feats of imagination, but before moving the examination along we must further investigate certain elements of our dilemma. Let us leave our discussion of the *AoP* with the following: man's weakness before the *AoP* ought to be assumed. This is not the same thing as saying that absolute power corrupts, for on one hand we are not talking about an actually "absolute" power (as in the absolute power of divinity, for example, instead we intend its meaning to be only absolute within its given constraints) and on the other, we have all observed the most inconsequential of dispensations produce, as a point of fact, corruption as overwhelming as the kind expected from those who wield truly meaningful influence. The skepticism towards power ought itself not be absolute; rather, we should hold the contemporary view of a universal and democratically distributed potential for power-holding with skepticism. An exclusionary concept of power would help us move our skepticism elsewhere, in more fruitful directions, but for now our investigation must take a minor detour.

13 "Manichaeism" refers to a worldview founded on the principle of conflict between Good and Evil.

"Hot" Politics and "Cold" Politics

In *Understanding Media,* Marshall McLuhan designated certain mediums (technology forms, or in McLuhan's own words, *"extensions of ourselves"*) as being either *"hot"*[14] or *"cold"*[15]. For McLuhan, the "form" (the medium as an extended sense or organ) is in fact the relevant unit of analysis and not the "content" (the message as some other extended sense or organ, in McLuhan's view itself another medium—the extension of a sense or organ via the extension of some other sense or organ), but man is typically too *dazzled* by the *magic of the message* to bother thinking about the *meaning of the medium.* I believe there is an application of this theory here, albeit in mutated form. [16] Phenomenologically, there are distinctions to be made between the *SoE* and the *PSoE* that a McLuhan-ite framing serves to make more coherent. Use of McLuhan's linguistic and conceptual framework also lets us fold in a specific dimension of the political which distinguishes our examination of the *SoE* from preceding ones, though we will be attempting a hybridization of his terms to further interrogate the origins of contemporary suspicion-culture.

The *SoE* is the hot medium of politics due to its highly saturating and detribalizing features. We may use the 2016 presidential election as an example to demonstrate. Whether appearing in a visual, auditory, or tactile medium, the message of Donald Trump neither asked nor demanded anything of its

14 Quoting McLuhan further, *"A hot medium extends one single sense in 'high-definition'. High definition is the state of being well filled with data. Hot media are, therefore, low in participation"*. Elsewhere, McLuhan describes high definition as *"engender[ing] specialism and fragmentation in living"* and *"detribalizing"*, and furthermore, that the *"hotting up of one sense tends to effect hypnosis"*.

15 Defined as *"low-definition"*, *"high in participation"*, *"retribalizing"*, with *"the cooling of the senses tend[ing] to result in hallucination"*.

16 Marshall McLuhan, *Understanding Media: The Extensions of Man*, First MIT Press Edition (Massachusetts Institute of Technology, 1994), 7, 22–24, 32.

consumer. At the first glimpse, the first hint, the first touch of Donald J. Trump, the consumer knew everything there was to know about him and his campaign. There was absolutely no ambiguity, no suspicious contrivance, nothing to be hinted at, pondered over, or analyzed. Prominent liberal agents and institutions worked hard to cast the opposite impression, and to a not insignificant degree the coercive social power generated by this effort did influence the thoughts and feelings of the Rightist electorate, though it was ultimately to no avail. He simply was, and *there he was* in a full-throated, colorful, vivacious, and exciting way. High-octane, yes, but high in informational content as well. Everyone knew what would happen with a President Trump because he told us so—repeatedly.

> *"You're going to be so proud of your country if I get in. You're going to be so proud of your president and I don't care about that. But you are going to be so proud of your country because we are going to turn it around. And we're going to start winning again. We're going to win so much, at every level, we're going to win economically, we're going to win with the economy, we're going to win with the military...we're going to win so much—you may even get tired of winning! And you'll say, 'Please, please, it's too much winning, we can't take it anymore. Mr. President, it's too much', and I'll say 'No it isn't, we have to keep winning. We have to win more!' We've got to win more!"*

Never once was there a question about what Donald Trump thought or intended, for he was so open and candid throughout his campaign. Or rather, that was the message conveyed by the Trump-medium. The American public did not need to project themselves into the man, just as they did not need to wonder if he would do them harm; they could simply bask in the warm, radiant glow of his charisma, secure in the knowledge that he would be their God-Emperor. No part of the Donald Trump message necessitated his audience filling in some blank or empty space; in fact, this has always been one of the greatest strengths of Donald Trump the medium. Now you may be asking, *"And what 'sense' was extended by Trump and his campaign?"*. Well, it was the sense of trust, and importantly, of paternalistic love: the return of the king, to put it in grandiose terms. It was right there in his smile, his voice, the way he would hug the American flag before delivering his speech. It was present, as well, in the size of his audience, the number of rallies he held, the aesthetic he presented on stage, right down to the signature red trucker hat. For those still skeptical I simply ask you to recall the single compliment most proffered by Trump supporters:

"He says what he thinks!"

For the average American there was simply no more to the equation than that. They were, as McLuhan observed of "hot mediums", *hypnotized.*

Conclusive as this may seem, we have yet more proof to examine. The other "hot" dimension of Trump's political campaign was the unquestionable air of separatism in every speech. Trump's campaign was detribalizing to the paradigm of global politics, global citizenry, and to the as-practiced-convention of mass society politics. From the point of view established earlier in this chapter, knowing that by 2016 America was operating well within the *PSoE* (and likely had been, in a more formal sense, since the time of the second Bush regime and its alleged "war on global terror"), this roaring reignition of national politics represented a clear off-script moment for the global technocratic order. The *charade* of politics threatened to become something more, it threatened to become what it always was, and slowly the whole country—and even the whole of our Western world—came to recognize that fact. For a time, anyway, the Trump message continually peeled people away from prevailing conventions, detribalizing them as consumers, as voters, and as citizens of the American empire. Most troubling of all (to the managers of terrestrial globalization,[17] that is) was the fact that the Trump-message threatened to separate America itself from the litany of trade agreements, pacts, and arrangements—all of which had long been assumed impervious to change.

Contrast this with the "cold" politics of the *PSoE,* which, as we have already discussed, is a consolidating and totalitarianizing political program, designed to retribalize the governed into the paradigm of *nR*. Because cold politics is definitionally incapable of enflaming the sense of trust, it engages a multiplicity of the electorate's senses (drawing them slowly into the hallucination that is *nR*). Both of Donald Trump's presidential opponents meet the criteria of "cold" political operators, as both *required* the voting audience to fill in the suspicious gaps left by the candidates and their campaigns. Hillary Clinton and Joe Biden, both being in abjectly poor health, left a lot to the imagination of the American voter. Not only were Democrat voters asked to draw their own conclusions about their candidate's relative fitness, but also their platforms! And their whereabouts! Much of their respective campaigns were about hiding the nominee from the American people. This would be the definition of a low-resolution or low-information political campaign. We might also think of Jeb Bush's infamous Clap-Gate scandal; cold mediums instigate the audience into participation, but in this case Jeb Bush *demanded* the audience's participation, thus making the form of cold politics explicit. Critical to the notion of "cold politics" (and, by extension, the *PSoE*) is the idea of compliance, and of conformity, as the state enjoins us to flatter and validate it (thereby inaugurating narcissistic co-dependency as a political style).

Earlier we claimed a phenomenological distinction existed between the two political conditions—a point to which we may now return. As a medium for totalitarianism (continuing

17 Peter Sloterdijk's choice of verbiage for the colloquially understood term, "globalism".

with the McLuhanite framework), which is itself a medium for deicide and of the Ego, the *PSoE* is not merely an extension into the political: it is an attempted extension into the metaphysical via transvaluation. A *PSoE* does not merely disorient the norms and mores of a given social order, nor is their influence limited to its development of an inverted eugenics. The *PSoE* is a program against the procession of time and history, and more significantly, it is a movement to blot out the very sky itself and prevent "real" divinity from entering this world.

So long as the *PSoE* reigns supreme, time stands still; we count the passing of seconds into hours, just as we commemorate the fulfillment of each year, but our clocks and calendars only keep track of stolen time—of the possibility of time, and all the time that could have been. We age, we decay, and the people we love (or simply desire to) all pass away, but because there is no time at all, there is also no time to mourn. With the advent of simulation technologies (the kinds we observe in popular Hollywood films or on some massive festival stage), there may in fact no longer be time to die. A beloved Hollywood starlet may pass tragically, only to reappear years later in digitized format, her image (no longer her own or even God's, for that matter) reconstituted time and time again to persist in perpetuity as a commodity form. Today it is digital Hollywood, tomorrow it is digital daughter, father, and lover. To a great degree this transformation has already come to pass, though it has not completely swept away the normative modes of social intimacy which preceded it. Under hypermodernity, death is not the end, merely an unfortunate speed bump along the way towards ultimate desacralization and commoditization. Thanks to the *PSoE*, quantified time wanes, agitates, leaps backward (under too intense an observation) or forward (under too loose a consideration), but above all—time never truly *happens*. The hypermodern *PSoE* conditions us to view the promise of "forever" as an imminent and existential threat.

Elimination of time negates the possibility of deep human

endeavoring and necessarily thrusts a people-group into despair and, thereafter, vice. Unable to know or touch God, what other condition *could* a tribe fall into? Contrast this with the saturation of time and divinity innate to the *SoE:* God enters the world, and with it into history through man and his obligation to act. Time within the *SoE* is, in a nearly literal sense, a time on fire. Specifically, it is an *animated* time characterized by the intense saturation (bordering on over-saturation) of information located in the moment-to-moment experiences of Man and his communal order.

(It should be noted that this dichotomy is not one of "better" or "worse", such that the individual events and outcomes for those enduring one state or the other are necessarily favorable or unfavorable depending on the condition of the state itself. People still die, suffer indignities, betrayals and the like, under the reign of an authentic power. A distinction between the two is found in the following fact: it is the aim of cool politics to convert tragedy into sardonic irrelevance. Tragedy occurs within the hot political order, but it is necessarily an honorable, integral tragedy—one which does not carry the same alienating trait as that of the "hotted up" *PSoE.*)

Within "hot" time, the time of the *SoE*, it is possible to live *more.* For all the transhumanist fervor about technologically extending human life (from a McLuhan-ite perspective, the obvious question would follow, *"Just what is getting extended into human life and how will that make a mess of our living traditions?"*), to say nothing of the general attitude of "increasing", "extending", and "enriching" life through dietary and surgical methods, we are never actually promised *more* life—only a *longer* one. Well, what good is an additional seventy years spent under the boot of some cold, totalitarian regime? Any good student of the human soul knows that it is the threat of forever which most fervently drives man to take his own life.

The saturation of time under a hot regime is such that one may fit an entire generation's worth of living into a single

36-month period. Saturated time naturally produces saturated memory and so the individual can easily recall their experience of living through a hot time well after the fact. Hot time is a manic, ecstatically religious time and as such it is also a time of justice, even retribution. The *PSoE* is committed to halting this, revanchist as it is, and so it suspends all life (or whatever is within its influence to achieve). Cold time is a punishing winter storming deep within the soul of Man, one that if not intervened upon, would spell the demise of his civilization.

"Arthurianism" versus "Faustianism"

At the climax of Christopher Nolan's 2008 film *The Dark Knight,* Heath Ledger's Joker launches a high stakes social experiment designed to prove the corruptibility of Man. He rigs two ferries with explosives (one containing convicts, the other civilians), all the while providing both parties with the means to destroy the other and save themselves. They are forced to choose, Joker instructs them, as both ferries will explode at a time of his choosing should either party fail to sacrifice the other. Joker's gamble fails on two fronts as neither ferry detonates their trigger, culminating in his arrest at the hands of the Batman (who then terminates the final detonation sequence).

Nolan tells us something very interesting about power through the character of the Joker. All throughout the movie, Heath Ledger's characteropenly flouts the vulgar power displayed by Gotham's criminal elite. In virtually every instance he successfully demonstrates that the very things they believe matter, that are both the causes of *and* the fruits of their influence, are in fact, completely worthless. Everything from their garish manner of dress to the strength of their bodyguards, to their money, to the advantages of operating outside legal jurisdiction—neither the symbols nor sources of their power saved them from the Batman, demonstrating that they were (and had been all along) powerless. Their successes, while certainly formidable, were ultimately incomparable to a force of nature like the Batman (and by the same logic, the Joker himself). In his final theatrical act of chaos, the Joker forced the city of Gotham to demonstrate what real power is and where it comes from. The Joker's experiment falls apart, not only affirming Man's essential goodness, but more importantly, its failure validates the sovereign authority's right to absolute power. Protectors of the law can, in fact, act with unrestrainedauthority and not merely descend into despotism. Not all overreaches are unjust, nor are they all permanent (a true *SoE*).

Naturally, the Batman's heroism takes narrative central stage; however, it is not the most, shall we say, *philosophically* compelling thread of the film's closing act. The tension between the two imperiled ferries, both locked in the same desperate struggle and yet isolated from one another, holds the key to the film's most striking message. Faced with the choice of life over death (and armed with the means to preserve themselves), only one man could stand up and act decisively. Only one man *knew* the Good and had the temerity to act on it. Certainly, all parties thought they knew what was right and moreover, were quick to let everyone else around them know it. Nolan shows us the reality of chaos. More importantly, he shows us how true authority emerges out of the chaos to seize power; the civilians invoke consensus, fret over "fairness", and rush to inept, impotent judgment while the convicts immediately resort to violence. We see the morality of two kinds of men stall and cancel the other out, each side "knowing" what was right but too afraid or otherwise unable to deliver it. This, of course, may have had to do with the fact that they *did not* know anything of the Good and were, instead, acting irrationally and out of hysterical fear. In the final moments of the sequence (and with time desperately wasting away), a truly authoritative man (a convict) steps forward: a man, presumably, with true knowledge of the Good (at the very least, he is a man with reverence for the power of life over death), who effortlessly dispatches their trigger, finally bringing the pandemonium to a close. God (at least, the God of Gotham, anyway) takes note of the courageous act, delivering the miracle which will save the lives of all and bring the Joker's anarchic reign to a close.

Nolan's scene is a dramatization of what I am calling *Arthurian* power, a concept which I am introducing in the hopes that it provides us with a model of authentic authority which, upon implementation, should drive the reversal of the *PSoE* and terminate production of suspicion-culture. Derived from the poem by de Boron,[18] wherein a young Arthur Pendragon miraculously claims his rightful identity and sovereignty as the true King of Britain, Arthurian power denotes the power of an authority as justified by the capacity to achieve acts of greatness which no other man is capable of, all the while performed in furtherance of his tribe. Only a boy at the time, Arthur successfully retrieved the sword Excalibur (prophesized to reveal the identity of the true king and son of Uther Pendragon), using it to forge his legacy as one of the greatest rulers in recorded British history. Arthurian power is the power immanent in genuine sovereignty, and thus the weapon of decision wielded during the *SoE*. Furthermore, it is a *shepherdly* power and stands in absolute contrast to the *tragic* power of Spenglerian Faustianism. I will elaborate this further, but a slight digression must be taken first.

In contemporary understanding and usage, "power" is the bastard son of influence, force, and will. Foggy a concept as can be, we speak a great deal of power but because we fail to distinguish one kind of power from the other, conflating all varieties of "Great Men" and their accomplishments into a single bloated Frankensteinian monster of uselessness, we remain ignorant of what power truly is. If we cannot speak correctly of authority as such, then we cannot possibly speak of cultivating an authority of our own. We may speak of the "power" of the Senate, the "power" of a singer's voice, or the "power" of

18 Robert de Boron, a 12th-13th century French poet who wrote a cycle of Arthurian Romances.

a roaring tidal wave without ever once speaking of the same thing.[19] Similarly, we speak of the "power" of the American military in the same language we speak of a popular athlete as a "power player" (here is one more: the stopping "power" of a bullet versus the show-stopping "power" of a theatre troupe). Democratization of power is one method of suppressing genuine sovereignty; flattening of both the avenues toward and discourse about power flattens its conceptual boundaries and retards the capacity for the average person to identify actual (or potential) sovereignty. The evaluative element of human consciousness descends into crass vulgarity, assessing sovereignty along subjective measures (as the possibility of any objective standard has already been eliminated). Real and enduring power is, as we have said, the power of life and death, and of creation and destruction. Real power enters the world through Man but does not originate within him. Real power is often exercised during the most terrible of dilemmas, forcing Man to act during the most nerve-wracking and impossible of circumstances. In other words, real power is something awful to behold.

As such, all other "expressions" of power are either simulacra, or simply lower order measurements of human achievement and influence (with "influence" serving as an appropriate "net" for capturing all lower order expressions of social capital). Force is often an element of power, and because of the frequency with which it is implemented, we see simulations of power (demonstrations of physical force) used at every level of social organization and justified as though they were authentic instances of miraculous decisiveness. Here is where elements of human conduct such as willfulness and desire enter the fray; people mistake *the fact* of successful displays of the

19 On the other hand, considering the examples provided they do in fact share a commonality: the impression, or sense of awe, which is stamped upon the consciousness of the observer. Of course, each kind of power strikes awe for differing reasons, bringing us back once more to the same dilemma of ambiguous non-differentiation.

will (or simple physical strength), as being synonymous with what we are here calling Arthurian (or actual) power. From the point of view of the estranged individual, himself feeling incapable of any will or desire at all, the disempowered person clings to simulacrum of power and simulations of authority, empowering himself through proximity to "greatness", and in the process validating the narcissism of simulated authority (and furthermore, jeopardizing the health of the social order in general by providing the "proof" of authentic authority in the eyes of confused passersby). My explanation is not a matter of simple mimesis, whereby the more people engage in some conduct the more it will persist, with the simplest and most vulgar methods of social ladder-climbing garnering the most approval, for in the mimetic model (at least Rene Girard's formulation of it) original desire plays no role in the matter[20]. For us, it plays a considerable role, for the entire performative charade is itself an external dramatization of internal self-perceptions and experiences, themselves generated by desire. Yes, it is true that many men lack an original fire, while a great many others spend their whole lives in pursuit of what Girard called "metaphysical desire", but these facts are not by themselves sufficient to expel desire from human psychology. Even in his imitation, Man has a way of making the desire of the other his own. Will and desire, being very closely related as devices for the organization and execution of human action, have less to do with genuine (Arthurian) power than they do more banal attempts at influence peddling. Arthurian power—we might also term it *shepherdly power*—makes an avatar of man, and as such, his own will is displaced by the presence of the divine will. Arthurianism holds close to its ownkind of desire: a sacred, righteous desire.

20 Rene Girard, a French anthropologist, historian, and literary critic, rose to prominence in 1961 on the merits of his "mimetic desire" hypothesis. His work on this subject led to perhaps his best-known accomplishment: the discovery of the "scapegoat mechanism".

Detour aside, the tragic power of Faustian Man is Icarian through and through, and therefore an inappropriate model of authentic authority, excellence, or generativity. Faustian Man's power is self-eliminating in its pursuit of the absolute limit of human existence. The story of Icarus, much like Goethe's portrayal of Faust, is rife with tragedy and death, the source of which is located within Man and his restless spirit. His frustration with human limitations (in the case of Faust), with confinements (in the case of Icarus), *his desire for more* (true of both) all condemn the strident and pioneering man to catastrophe. The tragedy of Icarian power, which is also the tragedy of the Faustian Man, is that the moment of defeat arrives at the pinnacle of his achievement or self-transcendence, leaving man with precious opportunity to savor the joy of self-overcoming before crashing to his doom. Tragic power, the power sought by Icarus and Faust, (a power which drives the present-day march of terrestrial globalization) is the power of Man-become-God (itself synonymous with the self-immolation of Man).

I am not establishing a dichotomy such that tragic power (Faustianism) is necessarily weaker, more ineffectual, productive of more negative outcomes than shepherdly power (Arthurianism), or that it is never Faustian Man riding in the driver's seat of the *SoE*. At least as far as the Spenglerian formulation is concerned, Faustianism is synonymous with the greatness of Western civilization; so strong is the association of Faustianism with Western excellence that few concerned with the question of civilizational flourishing even think to conceive of an alternative (itself a complicating factor for Arthurianism). Across the span of his singular life, man lives out that which the great hulking mass of his society lived over the period of many centuries, and in the spectacle driven hypermodern *TIS*, this means we can observe the Faustian cycle of tragi-power play out right before our eyes. We may draw two such examples from the very recent history of American popular culture to demonstrate the error of Faustian tragic power: Metallica and Michael Jackson. Metallica formulated their once-in-a-generation sound of metallic, "hot" Californian alienation and marched right into the *nR* of the recording industry with it, taking the country—and the world—by violent, head-banging storm.[21] While they were able to transform a four-album run into a lifelong *industry* which kept a great number of skilled people happily employed, their success came at expense of the lives and health of the band members themselves (and simultaneously resulted in the very death of the genre itself). In the case of Michael Jackson, we have something very different for—unlike Metallica—Michael Jackson was *born* of *nR* and not merely smuggled into it. All his life, Michael only knew the entertainment business, and his youth was dedicated to it (some might say, *sacrificed* to it). His achievements still stagger audiences around the world although it must be said (despite its obvious facticity), that the man used his wealth and fame to pursue the absolute limits of self-overcoming, possibly even to the detriment of his legacy as a recording artist and cultural figure. Tragi-power defines the career and consequences suffered by Michael Jackson every bit as much as it describes them for Metallica (even though their individual circumstances were quite different): broken families, dead band members, lawsuits, televised psychotherapy sessions, drug addictions, and soured legacies. Our desire for self-overcoming and self-transcendence, for progress and omnipotence masked our tolerance for the most depraved kinds of vanity and egotism.

Observers and critics alike make the very mistake McLuhan cautioned against when they overdetermine the meaning and value of the content (the music, their legacies) in relation to the form (the simulacra of culture production, the *nR* of the culture industry), in most cases ignoring the latter completely.

21 The recording industry being a simulacrum of culture production, though not a copy without an original, rather a copy that has supplanted the original, establishing a *nR* of culture production.

Enamored as we were, *dazzled* even by this technical and artistic brilliance, we never stopped to ask what the consequences of indiscriminately consuming electrically enhanced pleasure might be. Nor did we stop to think what consequences might arise from the promotion of an "at all costs" mentality of Faustian success and desire. At least our old Faustian heroes discovered new lands, invented new technologies, and carved out a world-historical legacy whose merits are still favorably argued today. The kind of vulgar and self-serving Faustianism, the desire to overcome local horizons rather than world-historical ones (for there are none remaining, thus rendering contemporary Faustian idealism farcical) promoted via the culture industry and indiscriminately accepted by the population at large, make a mockery of that which is truly great about our peoples and our history. So long as we remain ignorant of McLuhan's insight, we can only reify tragic power as the normative method of authority (and thus further the production of suspicion-culture).

Were these great Faustian figures mere men or Gods? Artistic figures or priestly ones? Is the goal for aspiring musicians to express themselves and hone their craft or to dominate the minds of men and women alike? To become who they truly are or to become vehicles of transmission for the aims and aspirations of a parasitical other? Does the culture industry create art or is it the artists themselves who are responsible? Do artists and musicians even need the culture industry? In so far as we even *ought* to speak of an artist's "career", the culture industry is a social-technological manifestation of Faustianism: Man achieves, strives for Godhood, fails, and then dies. Some time later, he is forgotten entirely. At least, that was Spengler's concern; so too is it our concern, today.

The same is true of the political world: are the political machines and institutions generative of authority or does genuine sovereignty arise from elsewhere? Or do our institutions quelch emergent greatness? The faux Faustianism which compels potentially great men to relieve themselves of their dignity and genuine strength for a fast-tracked path to political or cultural success—we can hardly compare it to the Faustian spirit of old, for Man is no longer selling his soul for anything other than mediocrity and the privilege to serve the least impressive and least worthy elites in living memory. Faustianism was always the devil's work, that much is undeniable. But these days, however, even the devil's labors strike us as impotent and without allure.

A final statement before we depart: let it also be said that the "shepherdly" power of Arthurianism is not necessarily less clever, less enterprising, or less robust than what we have seen from Faustian tragi-power. What Arthurianism provides is a narrative framework for the conception of a non-exploitative, non-desacralizing authority with deep roots in the authentic history of Western man's spirit, such that we may begin to re-orient ourselves to the *proper structure of authority itself* and propel the necessary ethnogenetic changes forward which will drive out the production of suspicion-culture.

Involuntary Immersion

We have said a great deal now about the political structure responsible for producing suspicion-culture, but by and large we have said little about the technological and psychological aspects of it or of its byproduct, conspiratorialism, at all. In the following chapter we will discuss the personality profiles of conspiratorially minded people and draw what relevant conclusions we may from them but as for now, let us continue to look at the problem of suspicion from a still broader and less individualized perspective.

It would be immensely helpful if McLuhan were with us today (or at the least, had produced a generation or two worth of acolytes) such that someone might be able to share with us the deep meaning of our present hypermodern moment of electronics and information. I do not get the impression that the essential contributions of his work have been well integrated, much less understood, and there remains a great many paradoxical elements within his ideas which complicate the deep assimilation of his model. Having said this, even a modest comprehension of his theoretical framework (such as my own) can still offer us a great insight into the technological and sociological dimensions of suspicion-culture.

Taking a McLuhanite view, the "global village" of the internet (the message of human consciousness, of the human nervous system shot across the globe through the medium of the electric light) whose message is itself an unending succession of mediums (each with their own message), ought to be considered a hot medium (so hot, in fact, that it effortlessly incinerates traditional modes of human endeavor), though the individual messages trafficked across it may not be as such. A classic hot medium stimulates a single sense in high-definition, which screen-mediated internet access still does, however in its characteristically hypermodern way, hot new media provides high-definition and high-resolution information to all senses all at once. New media content penetrates the immaterial, providing information that satisfies the deep abstract and meta-structure of desire. As such, the screen-mediated internet does not merely engross or hypnotize man (as McLuhan thought), rather it locks him into a state of total submission. Depending on the form of a given piece of internet-content, man is absorbed into it, subsumed by it, with only the variation of intensity and the nature of the sense-extension to differentiate them from one another. The internet *is* a web, and it *does* ensnare its users within it.

If we consider how much internet-content is consumed through the medium of the smart phone (which, as with the internet, is an innovation virtually synonymous with the hypermodern age), the way in which smart phone-mediated internet-content suspends rather than animates time (as well as, its intense capacity for retribalization, especially within multiracial democracies), it would be tempting to identify it with the order of "cold" politics. However, it is the "netted-ness" of wireless technology and the instantaneity with which it permits us to access information—these are accelerations which hasten (and *"heaten"*) the whole of the process. It is characteristic of hypermodernity that everything is *"that which it is, but a little more"* such that developments like the smart phone give us everything which previous technological iterations used to, but with an extra jolt added to the end of it. The mode of hypermodernity is synonymous with *over-accumulation* as much as it is *over-consumption* and so it is only natural that this would also be so with technology. That *"little more"* comes to us in many unexpected ways, though the one which interests us most is the *psychopolitical remainder* (more on that in just a moment, for now let us elaborate this point further).

The "unified sensorium" McLuhan attributed to the television has become a uniform feature of all messages within the *PSoE* via the regime of the screen. What was previously a cooler and lower-information medium now radiates heat thanks to the hypermodern addition of *choice*. When you can specialize the content without end, as hypermodernity permits, then the problem of "low resolution" and "low information" content completely disappears (and where it does not disappear, then all previous assumptions and beliefs about it disappear in the face of this new context). The internet as a medium of decentralization is therefore the medium of specialization par excellence, and as such all content which passes through it gets "hotted up" on the way to its destination. Here we see where advancements made within our time, advancements that could not have been anticipated during McLuhan's age, require us to make certain corrections to the model if we are to put it to work for our time. The ascent of neoliberal hypermodernity also brought along with it, as we know, a program of intensified self-interest in the individual, his interests, and his proclivities; in short, the state has become both friendlier and more accommodating in its method for extracting compliance from the governed (here I am speaking of Hungarian psychiatrist Thomas Szasz's concept of "the therapeutic state", which grounds our interest in "psychopolitics"). Media is *more about the consumer* than ever before, and especially, *about the effect which new media is intended to have* on the consumer. To secure greater compliance, to extract more information from (and about) the consumer, to penetrate more rapidly into his deep soul, to convey the absolute malice and nihilism of the content creators (and providers)—these are some of the ways in which both the message and the medium have changed under hypermodernity. Setting aside all arguments provided so far about the nature and production of suspicion-culture, *the very fact of this intensified interest itself* is sufficient to produce widespread suspicion. The images, associations, sounds, and ideas brought to consciousness through this new medium are, themselves, literally beyond belief.

The screen, having risen to dominance since its inception, turns the volume up on all sense experiences in accordance with the mandate for *more*. Screens deliver messages of every kind, messages which are increasingly an assault on all senses, as the purpose of media in the *PSoE* is no longer strictly participative or even absorptive as such, but anaesthetization. The screen, also a medium for the transmission of the psychopolitical, *does in fact* disseminate low-information content, though as we have said this is not specifically a problem for the hypermodern regime (for there is no longer even the pretense of rational transmission, let alone exchange). Of course, this may be a material consequence of operating within a multiracial democracy, but all the same, the shift to direct emotional manipulation (as opposed to the indirect manipulation of earlier periods) reflects a change in the application of influence (and, as well, a change in the relation between consumer and producer). It is a change specifically deriving from the mandate of the *PSoE*). The electric net of human consciousness makes the extension of all things through all other things possible, creating a residue and a stain, a contamination which smears itself across the whole of media. All of society is made to carry the psychic brunt of those who control our media-forms.

Suspicion-culture is also the result of the ongoing paradoxicalizing of life. ("*We took all of our data digital and now we have power failures in the office all the time*"; "*The people I feel closest to are the farthest away from me*"; "*I can have all the sex that I want with as many configurations of people as I want and yet I do not feel pleasure*", etc.) Suspicion of this form is the suspicion of having been taken for a ride (a suspicion which rapidly turns to resentment—resentment for believing in the people who told them "*This is a good deal*"). This restlessness (ennui being yet another wonderful byproduct of hypermodernity), the form taken up by the ever-escalating pitch of tension (caused, as we have said, by the endless multiplication and intensification of paradoxes) contributes to the profound and heart-wrenchingly ubiquitous sense of joylessness which is foundational to the present production and sustenance of suspicion-culture. We should say here, though, that this is merely one method for producing the mass experience of joylessness which plagues daily life in America. (To this point we will return in the next section.)

The relative decentralization of and "liberty" afforded to Americans, in tandem with the democratization of access to ever sophisticating technological forms created the material conditions for what I am calling "*involuntary immersion*". Involuntary immersion occurs when an individual undergoes a "depth experience" (an intense and meaningful instance of engrossment) after interacting with some technological hyperworld, such that they have experienced clinically significant and persistent derealization. A cognition-form endemic to this condition is one which I call "*conspiracizing*", the affective consequence of which we shall dub "*illegitimate suspicion*". Now it is generally good form to avoid the unnecessary production and multiplication of terms, but unfortunately when it comes to the question of "the conspiracy theory" (and more importantly, "the conspiracy theorist"), we are left wanting for rational discourse and thus we construct our own from the ground up. Conspiracizing is a form of paranoid catastrophizing and conjecturing, the object of which is in fact a *hyperobject* (a non-local entity) and thus—at least initially—distal, remote, and not of immediately or reasonably justifiable importance. Over time individuals stricken with despair will seek to bridge the hypermodern gap between themselves and their hyperobject of choice, even if doing so could prove fatal. Illegitimate suspicion, which is both the engine and effect of this process, is a psychic contaminant which erodes the trust necessary to produce joy and secure our daily way of life. We will speak more of illegitimate suspicion elsewhere, but suffice to say, we may describe it as the undue and precedent-less application of doubt directed at some person or event. When we speak of "hyperpolarization" we are often speaking of this phenomenon.

It is not a necessary consequence of internet exposure, though for a small and clinically distinct percentage of the population it may be typical; rather, it is the fact of Imperial America's teleological shift and the alienation which it produces (to say nothing of the tremendous physical destruction of communities caused by the same shift) that drives people to seek refuge in the hyperworld of the internet and lose capacity to answer the demands of day-to-day life. Disbelief in the events and doctrines of the lifeworld (the actual world of shared social experiences and meanings) are magnified by this submersion into the hyperworld (the simulacrum world of technological origin, e.g., the internet) and then reintroduced into the lifeworld, having been "psychoticized" by the combinatory punches of technological development, political disenfranchisement, and social estrangement.

We observe three instances (significant ones, at that) of

involuntary immersion and its political consequences below:

1. While QAnon as a political medium "hotted" up American discourse (and even the White House front lawn), QAnon as a fascination and a message feverishly consumed through computers and smart phones was a rather *"cool"* affair. QAnon the message retribalized the electorate into conventional, consumptive, uni-party Conservatism, thus retarding the sudden and inconceivable political growth made during the "hot" primary. QAnon the message undermined QAnon the medium with its cold and cryptical "Q drops": indigestible nuggets of information supposedly left like breadcrumbs guiding overzealous patriots toward political utopia. Having already undergone introjection, QAnon demanded even more of them than and their support than Donald Trump ever did; to participate with the "cold" message of "Q", these fine patriotic Americans had to vomit back up this psychic reformulation, their *nu-Self* (the newly constructed identity—part Trump, part authentically their own), and deposit it squarely into the holes "Q" certainly must have intended to fill with substantive information. The conservative tendency for dogged-and-irrational loyalty (in conjunction with the cognitive reality of the sunk cost fallacy), would have been more than enough to castrate the nascent MAGA movement but the "hotted" up neoliberal intelligence community was not content to let the scene play itself out to its natural conclusion. *"Involuntary immersion"* occurred among what would later become Trump's electorate because of the increased "hotting up" of America, driving tens of millions of Americans into different habits and sources of information

and entertainment consumption (while driving untold numbers out of consumption altogether). American imperial teleology's shifting goal posts had produced "dormant dissidents" of every kind with such alarming regularity that the *TIS* had slept walked into a truly world historical *SoE*. The collision of digitally mediated mediums, from the hot forms such as Twitter (the medium of print), Instagram (the medium of photography), and the podcast (the medium of radio), to cold forms like Facebook (a blended medium, but no doubt cold) and YouTube (the medium of television) served as the technological fuel for the extension of Donald Trump into the central nervous system of every voting-aged American.

2. The 9/11 truth movement, too, was a "hot" political movement, one that for a short time served as a wellspring of tremendous political radicalization culminating, arguably, in the *Occupy* movement. Aspects of the 9/11 truth movement frustrated well-to-do liberals (notably Jon Stewart, then host of *The Daily Show*) who wanted to express conventional and sanitized critiques of the wars in Iraq and Afghanistan (and the George W. Bush administration in general) without invoking the genuine resentment of people who had scratched just a little deeper under the skin of the issue. Against the backdrop of literate liberal society, high-speed internet use ushered in a wave of rationalism, empiricism, and skepticism best exemplified in the Comedy Central program "*The Daily Show*", the New Atheist movement, and the various talking heads of the YouTube community. Or that is, it ushered in the *image* of these things. With the aid of the "hotted up television" of YouTube came

the even "hotter" message of documentary film, where titles like *Loose Change*, *Zeitgeist*, and *Fahrenheit 9/11* (a more conventional entry than the two previously mentioned, admittedly) initiated naïve, bored, and paranoid Americans alike into a still nascent form of digital esotericism. Both the last gasp of an originary suspicion-culture and the genesis of a fresh (and farcical) repetition, this *SoE* would spawn wave after wave of commoditized esoteric digi-cults. Regardless of how it ended, millions of Americans had scratched well beneath the surface and ended up radicalizing (or catastrophizing, usually the latter) themselves into mass political demonstration. The naked tyranny of the Bush regime, exposed in real time within the space of the only-just-emerging hyperworld, shattered the minds of a great many people. Liberal America was so enflamed with righteous anger that it promptly voted a half-Black man into the office of the Presidency out of resentment (and then bragged about it for the next decade). This hot detribalizing of White Liberals has driven American politics ever since.

3. Which brings us, of course, to "BlueAnon", the great inheritor of Bush-era hotted up liberal suspicion-culture. Detribalized by the media war waged against then President W. Bush on behalf of the liberal establishment, White liberal America was retribalized over the coming years into a new community, an international community—that of the neoliberal open society. A shadow parallel of the QAnon movement, rhetorically "hot" while politically "cold" (destabilizing to the integrity of civic unity but at the same time, stabilizing—or containing—the liberal voting bloc), Russiagate/

BlueAnon (and the related anti-populist narratives deployed by the neoliberal establishment in conjunction with the intelligence communities) stymied populist conservatism's remarkable ascent to political power. The Russiagate/BlueAnon incident illustrated quite well what I have called "hypermodern suspicion-culture", which to summarize only briefly (we will return to this concept in the third chapter) is founded in irrationalist anti-empiricism and solipsism. Like the QAnon movement, BlueAnon was not rooted in factuality; while QAnon traded on faith, that is, a patriot's faith in truth, justice, and the indomitability of Goodness, the anti-Trumpist conspiracies which coalesced around Russiagate/BlueAnon were driven by the most audacious kind of anti-factuality, rooted not in faith but in self-aggrandizement and ego-inflation. Both movements manipulated the despair of their targets: in the case of QAnon and Trumpist America, their despair was colored by the realization that civility and national camaraderie were suddenly, silently, rendered null and void. As for the liberal "resistance", their despair could be found in the fact that the open society's revisioning of America was not complete, and furthermore, that such a completion may no longer be possible. America's intractable and shameful history of nativism would not fade into the collective rearview mirror, instead, it appeared ready to reassert itself, in effect dispelling liberal America's perceived cultural victories (secured, as they were, during the two-term reign of neoliberalism's greatest hero: Barack Obama. Both movements, (QAnon and "the resistance") served a therapeutic function, to ameliorate the anxieties of a suddenly alert and activated political population, one marked by complacency (conservatism) while the other, ruthlessness (progressivism).

21st Century Schizoid Man

Depending on your temperament, either the most fascinating aspects of Freud's work were to be found in the rigor and intensity of his thought, or in the casual and almost carelessly-thrown-out observations etched across his many works. I am somewhere in the middle, of course, but his remark (which I am paraphrasing here) about the "poet preceding the scientist and philosopher alike" continues to ring true. Consider the lyrics to King Crimson's "*21st Century Schizoid Man*" (taken from their debut album, "*In the Court of the Crimson King*", released in October of 1969):

Cat's foot iron claw
Neuro-surgeons scream for more
At paranoia's poison door
21st century schizoid man
Blood rack, barbed wire
Politician's funeral pyre
Innocents rapes with napalm fire
21st century schizoid man
Death seed, blind man's greed
Poet's starving, children bleed
Nothing he's got he really needs
21st century schizoid man.

At least from a psychiatric point of view, for many the commonly conceived image of the suffering and unintelligible man is that of the schizophrenic. This is doubly true when we think of the conspiratorial and suspicious man, himself being plagued by voices and images, and thus consumed by all manner of perceived threats and persecutions. The "tinfoil hat wearing freak" who only drinks water which he has personally strained of fluoridated molecules; the quiet, retired divorcee who takes up causes of suspicion because "the television" or "the dog" told him to; the woman who tracks the movement of the clouds in anticipation for the return of her alien lover and their small children; whenever we think of the conspiratorial and the suspicious, we are enjoined to think in these ways. Of course, such a demand is generally a demand to make suspicion itself seem ridiculous, declassee, and when necessary—flat out wrong and ill. But it is also a demand to ignore the societal-wide mass production of more systemic dysfunction—namely the inculcation of a sub-clinical grade schizoidal social affect upon the whole of American life. Industrial strength joylessness and self-interrogation, those blessed rewards of American citizenship, stir the phenomenological stew of suspicion (after all, the surest way to get someone to doubt those around is by getting them to doubt themselves first).

Enforcement of *nR* is synonymous with the schizotizing of America, for this implantation of law into American social consciousness simultaneously effects an implantation into the actual consciousness of individual Americans themselves. The result is akin to Laing's concept of *"the divided self"* and so on this subject I will let his words speak for themselves.

> Yet it has been remarked how charged with hostility is the self-scrutiny to which the schizoid subjects himself. The schizoid individual (and this applies still more to the schizophrenic) does not bask in the warmth of a loving self-regard. Self-scrutiny is quite improperly regarded as a form of narcissism. Neither the schizoid nor the schizophrenic is narcissistic in this sense. As a schizophrenic put it (see p. 204), she was scorched under the glare of a black sun. The schizoid individual exists under the black sun, the evil eye, of his own scrutiny. The glare of his awareness kills his spontaneity, his freshness; it destroys all joy. Everything withers under it. And yet he remains, although profoundly not narcissistic, compulsively preoccupied with the sustained

> observation of his own mental and/or bodily processes. In Federn's language, he cathects his ego-as-object with mortido.[22]

Laing continues in the following paragraph,

> A very similar point was made in different terms when it was said earlier that the schizoid individual depersonalizes his relationship with himself. That is to say, he turns the living spontaneity of his being into something dead and lifeless by inspecting it. This he does to others as well, and fears their doing it to him (petrification). We are now in a position to suggest that whereas he is afraid not to be dead and lifeless – as stated, he dreads real aliveness – so also he is afraid not to continue being aware of himself. Awareness of an object lessens its potential danger. Consciousness is then a type of radar, a scanning mechanism. The object can be felt to be under control. As a death ray, consciousness has two main properties: its power to petrify (to turn to stone: to turn oneself or the other into things); and its power to penetrate. Thus, if it is in these terms that the gaze of others is experienced, there is a constant dread and resentment at being turned into someone else's thing, of being penetrated by him, and a sense of being in someone else's power and control. Freedom then consists in being inaccessible..[23]

For us it is the implantation of the law which divides the self; the production of the schism causes the individual to endure "ontological insecurity" (another of Laing's concepts) by challenging both the past (his or hers deep learning) and the present (their very perceptions). While the schizophrenic is irreconcilable with society, the schizoid is not; schizoids may bear the brunt of cosmic doubt with the only casualty being the possibility of their own life's fulfillment, whereas the schizo-

22 R.D. Laing, *The Divided Self* (Tavistock Publications, 1959), p. 112.

23 Ibid, pg. 113.

phrenic, under the weight of the same doubt, recedes from social consensus altogether. Again, it is important to clarify that we are not speaking of a conventional, clinical grade schizoid personality disorder writ large, but of a persistent and agitating inflammation of "schizotism": inflation of the native capacity for suspicion via the implantation of a censor (self-negation).

A man feels he has no joy and because he feels as such, he accepts it as his fate. A stranger sees this man in his suffering, sees him preoccupied with it, observes him mired in his compulsiveness and decides that the suffering man deserves his joylessness—that it is, in fact, his own authentic misery. The first man, having seen his own disgust and contempt reflected in the gaze of the stranger, accepts the penetrating, suspicious glare as proof of his own innate (*and original*) dysfunction. Hypermodernity turns the heat up on this dynamic by the mass incorporation of *screens* and *content;* the screen is an extension of the eye and the gaze (and thus also of desire), and whereas the gaze of one man into another can only silently affirm the recipient's self-incinerating suspicion, the screen provides a discrete and continuous beam of suspicion-content which the viewer may then take up as his own (and add to, or intensify, his collection of existing suspicions). The imposition of desire, itself a compulsory mimesis, drives the wedge of suspicion somewhere into the recesses of Man's mind, depositing itself in virtue's nadir (free to reproduce and take up residence within as many other domains of existence open to it). Suspicion-mediums may take any form (we have discussed the significant ones already) but suspicion-messages (or suspicion-content, as we have used elsewhere) always seek to induce or implant one (or more) of the following:

1. A trace (as in a residue, a mark, an amount, or a stain; it is some visible remainder or proof left because of ingesting some suspicion-content), or
2. A cautious distrust (an ambiguous feeling directed at some person, place, group, or cause), or

3. A condemnation (an invitation to accuse some party of wrongdoing), or
4. A confirmation (an invitation to reconsider previously discarded, or perhaps unexamined, horrors; "confirmations", such as we are calling them, usually refer to the individual's paranoid feeling of being, or potentially being, persecuted. It may or may not be legitimate.)

Suspicion-content of the likes seen in advertisements enjoins the viewer to disbelieve their own material contentment, security of social status, or commitment to some *TIS*-sanctioned ideology or program. Advertisement and marketing-based suspicion-content may achieve all four of the outcomes discussed above. Entertainment-based suspicion-content usually strives for outcomes 1–3; the overall sophistication of entertainment has declined and therefore lacks both the intellect and the imagination necessary to achieve 4. Individuals who demonstrate the greatest susceptibility to 4 display a palpable level of total self-capitulation such that they are not capable of producing their own suspicion but are merely a conduit for the grander, civilizational architects of suspicion themselves. Formal political propaganda and rhetoric is similarly debased, achieving comparable outcomes to entertainment-based suspicion-content. The only way to achieve "confirmation" (4) among those segments of the population who are *not* paradigmatically compromised, such as I am aware, is in situations of either…

1. Identification or introjection with a producer of suspicion-content, or
2. Profound debilitation of the individual's self-evaluative faculty.

Effectively, "confirmations" are secured either by trust or through vice, a fact which casts a dark cloud upon the whole of the endeavor. Cynicism, a yet under-discussed precursor to suspicion-culture, is this dark cloud which makes trust and camaraderie appear forlorn and otherworldly. On this point, however, we must suspend further investigation and return to the discussion proper (though there will be an opportunity to resume our investigation into cynicism before reaching our conclusion).

We had begun to speak about joylessness, and to that we now return. Man experiences his joylessness as a kind of suction or vacuum, pre-emptively draining all feelings of love, camaraderie, and joy before they even enter his field as possibilities. Over time, it will drain him (or her) of the will to live entirely. Technically speaking, schizoids do not often attempt suicide; however, we are not speaking of a clinical schizoid disorder wherein the individual is in some sense "built" or "prepared" to carry such a burden. Schizotism is the introduction of an intolerable division into the minds and souls of normatively developed, neurotypical individuals, who by their very nature are not *"equipped"* to accommodate psychic neighbors such as these. If they do not outright take their own lives, because of the introduction of suspicion-culture, they will consciously elect to "self-terminate" in some other way (e.g., childlessness, drug abuse, self-barbarism, *et cetera*). Let us focus on this idea of self-barbarism. Schizotism is tantamount to self-barbarism and in fact this is the entire point. The *PSoE* makes containment a formal political operation, as that which requires containing are those psychic and social forces which would drive the reversal of affairs, a return of the king so to speak. So, what then are these forces which executors of the *PSoE* seek to contain? Bluntly stated, the answer is *brutality*. All the brutalist tendencies native to Man (e.g., vengeance-seeking, territoriality, bewilderment, madness, and so on) may be cultivated and directed by organized political opposition against the reign of *nR*. This potential reversal of affairs is understandably intolerable to the architects of *nR* and so they turn Man's brutalist instincts against himself through the legal and mass cultural imposition of *schizotism*.

Self-brutality makes the "*schizotized*" individual, in the words of Ernst Kretschmer, "*pliable*". This condition of being pliable renders the individual vulnerable to all manner of dysfunction, from the sexual and interpersonal to the chemical and psychiatric. If we view certain dysfunctions, in particular the forms of dysfunction which are enshrined as "virtuous", within *nR*, not from the lens of conventional psychological and sociological models but from our *psychopolitical* lens, they begin to look very different. Consider sexual dysfunction—BDSM for instance—in the light of our "*pliable schizotism*" theory: permissive neoliberal psychiatry does not attempt to scratch beneath the surface of this compulsion, content as it is to handwave it away with appeals to "consent", "self-exploration", and "self-expression". Sadism and violence, increasingly becoming the norm for sexual fantasies and conduct, can only be said to operate in a "consensual" manner if the individual in question has undergone depersonalization and self-objectification. The desire for brutality, impermissible as it has become, is no longer pursued as an external good but as an internal good, directed as we know at the body (the mechanism through which the self suspends, albeit temporarily, division). Violence itself is how schizotized individuals mend the dissolution of formal, stable consciousness, and today, violence is increasingly normative within interpersonal relations. Is it a natural desire, an expression of some authentic self, which compels man and woman alike into modes of sexual sadism (whether directly admitted or not), as neoliberal psychiatry enjoins us to believe, or is it a byproduct of the internal censor, observing and judging the whole of their development, damning them to a hell of the here-and-now? Violence does for the schizotized individual much the same thing that substance use, body modification, and other extreme activities do—it produces something akin to joy. Instances of cathartic violence are then concretized, their preceding events narrativized, and the whole of the event subject to therapeutic paralogisms which, when taken together, negate the attempted escape from consciousness (which was the point of the whole violent cathartic affair in the first place). What, on the outside, may seem like narcissistic navel-gazing, is in fact the feedback loop created by this behavior. Reassimilation of the *"schizotic"* man and woman is non-negotiable.

We might also say *"manipulable"* when we speak of *"pliable schizotism"*; in his schizotized condition, man is no different from a piece of furniture—something to be moved around at the leisure of others. As such, he may find himself in any number of contexts and thus susceptible to an enumerable instance of compulsions. The eccentricity often associated with formal schizoid suffering individuals is mimicked by the internet-addicted *"schizotic"* individual, for the atomizing lifestyle forced upon him by the *TIS* economically and politically reproduces the same self-isolating and niche fulfillment-seeking behaviors seen in conventional schizoids. It is not necessary to account for each expression and permutation of schizotism, only to highlight the fact of its self-brutalizing nature. The internal grind of suspicion and violence all but precludes any kind of existential transvaluation. A simpler way of describing this phenomenon would be to describe it as *self-negation.* Self-negation is akin to a counter-will (not to be understood in a strictly Rankian sense); embedded within the soul is a will counterposed to itself, counterposed to its own will to life, relentlessly driving the self-negating individual into repeated interpersonal conflict[24]. The counterwill makes him a liability both to himself and his tribe. It also, importantly, makes him a

24 Otto Rank, a Jewish-Viennese psychoanalyst and lifelong colleague to Sigmund Freud, first proposed the notion of a "counter-will" to explain the individual's innate psychological resistance to external coercion. Counter-will as used here is closer in meaning to Freud's "death instinct" though the two are not identical.

supplicant of neoliberal democracy.

Social Engineering as a Means for Stifling Political Dissent and Disrupting Folk Discourse

An obvious problem posed to those states which rely on deceit and suppression to manage their populations is that such conduct provokes dissent (obviously). States which militate against their own stock create for themselves a circumstance in which they will need to continually administer solutions, coercions, distractions, and other such means for preventing the emergence of an organized revolutionary consciousness. The result, then, is a kind of political arms race between what we may call *the folk account of history* and *the consensus (or regime) account of history*. A more exacting definition of these concepts will be provided in the third chapter, where they will be fleshed out more fully. Suffice to say, I invoke these terms to describe the phenomenon whereby the efforts of the state against the population instigate a movement by the population against the state, which is repeated *ad infinitum*, so on and so forth until some more *final* resolution arises. Folk populations view attempts at state expansion with intense scrutiny, meeting such developments with their own forays into autarky (which naturally provokes an immune response from the state). Infamous moments from our own history bear this dynamic out: Ruby Ridge in 1992, Waco in 1993, the Bundy standoff in 2014. While not all such confrontations end in bloodshed, they all speak to the increasing sense of irreconcilability between the regime (neoliberal democracy) and its victims (the folk).

Presently, the terms of this conflict are dictated by the open society, the one-time philosophical concept turned international political program. Karl Popper, its architect, argued fiercely for the need to defend the open society against barbaric and retrograde alternatives (e.g., fascism, communism, nativism, *et cetera*), going so far as to encourage the intentional and ongoing implementation of certain social engineering strategies to prevent any political alternative from ever arising. This is the present formulation of the *PSoE*, having emerged from the aftermath of the Second World War and remains to this day as the sole surviving model of political and social organization.

Popper had his acolytes—some were avowed (George Soros, for instance, his former pupil and eventual founder of the Open Society Foundation), while others were merely his spiritual successors. One such informal adherent—Cass Sunstein (though Sunstein does make direct reference to Popper in his writings) —famously applied Popper's model of piecemeal engineering (smaller scale interventions, applied only as needed) to behavioral economics, popularizing "nudge theory" as an alternative to the more coercive models of social policymaking which had been implemented up to that point[25][26]. By controlling the amount of information presented to an individual as well as the context in which it is presented, Sunstein aimed to directly influence the decision-making processes of the public. So well received were his ideas that both the US and the UK's governments created taskforces to apply Sunstein's work. While his nudge theory has wide-ranging applications, Sunstein's primary focus has long been to deter and disarm anti-regime thought.

I will critique Popper's social theorizing more directly in the third chapter, but for now let us approach it more obliquely (and contemporarily) through the medium of Cass Sunstein, whose work has been of monumental importance in shaping the regime's response to folk suspicion-culture, particularly the emergent *digital* suspicion-culture. For this portion of the analysis, I will be relying on the writings of Michael Collins Piper, a well-known and prolific researcher of conspiracies. In

25 Thaler, R. H., & Sunstein, C. R. (2012, October 4). *Nudge*. Penguin UK.

26 Sunstein, C. R., & Vermeule, A. (2008, January 1). *Conspiracy Theories*. Social Science Research Network. https://doi.org/10.2139/ssrn.1084585

his book *False Flags: Template for Terror* (from which I will now be quoting somewhat liberally) Piper identifies Sunstein as playing a central role in combating the rise of "conspiracy theories":

> At that time, one Cass Sunstein, a professor at the University of Chicago, and his co-author, Harvard law professor Adrian Vermeule, put forth a so-called "preliminary draft" of what was officially issued as "Harvard Public Law Working Paper No.08-03 and University of Chicago Public Law Working Paper No. 199". Although little-noticed at the time it was first issued, the "working paper" came under broad-ranging public inspection (widely discussed on the Internet) after Sunstein was drafted in 2009 by President Barack Obama to serve as administrator of the Office of Information and Regulatory Affairs, a post Sunstein departed in 2012.
>
> Later published under other auspices under the title "Conspiracy Theories," the paper addressed the specific question of how the government should respond to conspiracy theories that were now holding wide sway (particularly on the Internet) and, in no uncertain terms, addressed what Sunstein (who is Jewish) considered the specific danger of the growing belief that Israel had played a part in 9-11. Naturally, 9-11 truthers were outraged by this paper and noted (rightly so) that the co-author was now effectively "minister of information" for the Obama regime: A U.S. government official was actually pondering, in writing, how government power could be used to deal with conspiracy theories and those who believed in them![27] (p. 282).

Piper is correct to express concern over the fortuitousness of Sunstein's appointment to the Obama administration, for with Sunstein we see a certain habit—present, also, in Karl Popper's work—of particularity impersonating, or masquerading, as

27 Michael Collins Piper, *False Flags: Template for Terror* (America First Books, 2019), Ch. 29.

universality. That is to say, a cause is taken up under the pretext of preserving democracy, defending civic rights, or "countering extremism" to hide the fact of the agent's true motivation: paranoid self-preservation. In a way, Sunstein is merely upholding the oldest and most characteristic tradition of the open society (self-preservation) by framing his concerns over the threat posed by "conspiracy theories" in global terms. Despite this universalist framing, Sunstein betrays himself by quickly linking skepticism of the narrative around the September 11th attacks to Holocaust denial, and ultimately, the JFK assassination (for which a strongly plausible folk account implicates the Israeli State as co-conspirators). In passing, Sunstein mentions other prominent conspiracy theories, admitting the veracity of quite a few in the process. The fact of the folk account's existence, and importantly of its *potency*, troubles Sunstein. He argues that the state must intervene to disrupt it:

> The intriguers effectively determined that "if you can't lick 'em, join 'em" (as the old saying goes). That is, rather than working to REFUTE conspiracy theories, the solution would be to INFECT them and MISDIRECT them and add utter confusion to the mix. The consequence would be that conspiracy theories would look so ridiculous that no broad swath of people in the general public might one day actually begin to have any belief in their credibility.
>
> In the past, people did have doubts about the official stories relating to the JFK assassination, the Oklahoma City bombing and the 9-11 tragedy. Now, however, emerging alternative theories about other events would be totally eviscerated—from within—and die by their own accord. Anyone putting forth any form of conspiracy theory would automatically become suspect, their very sanity questioned.(p. 281).

While the liberal establishment remembers the two-term Obama presidency too fondly, proudly touting its supposed lack of controversies, in truth his administration provided lots of fodder for the conspiratorially minded to chew on. In a sense, conspiratoriality *defined* his presidency, as the question of Obama's very existence and origins lent themselves to a not-unreasonable scrutiny (a scrutiny that White, Right America nervously, nauseously, tip-toed around—desperate to speak freely but too terrified to do so). Two events, however, gave Piper reason to believe that Sunstein's policy efforts were being implemented in real time:

> The multiple streams of Internet provocations that captured the imagination of the "patriot" and "alternative" media following the Sandy Hook affair and the events in Boston were—beyond any question—the work of high-level conspirators whose designs were clear:
>
> 1. To monitor the reaction of known (and potential) political dissidents to public events of a "crisis" nature;
> 2. To gauge the level of conspiracy theorizing (and the acceptance of the theories) following such events;
> 3. To trace the origins of conspiracy theories and to chart their course via Internet websites, email and other social media venues;
> 4. To disrupt and misdirect conspiracy theorists and conspiracy theories whose views were deemed in some way problematic; and
> 5. To have in place a fully-functioning Crisis Management System— a very real "conspiracy"—that could be utilized to its fullest capacity at some future time.
>
> The first public hint of what was openly-acknowledged high-level intrigue of this sort—designed to undermine the 9-11 truth movement (not to mention any and all suggestions of conspiracies in other realms) was formally unveiled on January 15, 2008. (p. 281).

Piper continues later by saying:

> To those who understand Sunstein's proposition on the deeper level of Mind Control that it represents and who have likewise taken the time to carefully study the

> bigger picture in retrospect, it is all too apparent that the Internet-based frenzy following the Sandy Hook affair was clearly the work of the Sunstein crowd—we'll call them the Crisis Management Conspirators—who remembered all too well what Gustave Le Bon had said when he wrote so succinctly: "To know the art of impressing the imagination of crowds is to know at the same time the art of governing them."
>
> The Sandy Hook affair was tailor-made for putting the Sunstein gang's experiment in motion. It involved violence. It involved the explosive issue of gun control, inasmuch as the incident was said to have been a mass shooting. And it was another sensational school shooting—and one at a grade school, no less.
>
> The dynamics were absolutely on target—no pun intended—for the Sunstein thesis to be put to the test. And, quite predictably, the mass media—as a consequence of its typically reckless nature—played right into the scheme. The frenzied rush in the heat of the moment to get "the scoop" led to sloppy, reporting and presumably otherwise honest mistakes by journalists. And naturally, a lot of these errors were quickly the subject of discussion among emailers and those participating on Internet discussion forums who were concerned about the obvious push for further gun control that was accompanying the media reportage relating to the events at Sandy Hook. (p. 288).

Part of Sunstein's program, Piper argued, is the direct manipulation of language intended to limit the range and scope of any conspiratorial discourse. Of this, Piper says:

> But aside from the mis-reporting in the major media (whether deliberate or otherwise) it was almost exclusively on the Internet—via the so-called "truther" and "alternative" and "independent" websites, discussion groups, along with email and the popular video forum, YouTube, etc.—that a wide variety of absolutely baseless (and largely nonsensical) stories about Sandy

> Hook began to appear.
>
> This was clearly the work of a small but skilled team of operatives working for Sunstein and company. As Sunstein had suggested in his now-infamous working paper, their purpose was to manipulate—and ultimately refute—and make fools of—sincere truth seekers and so-called "conspiracy theorists."
>
> And, even more so, Sunstein's goal was to convince the broad range of the American public that anyone who spoke about any conspiracies at high levels was just simply not someone to be believed. One of the first and most outrageous of these Internet "revelations" that did so much to make sincere truth seekers look foolish was the oft-repeated theme that "Sandy Hook was a hoax" and that no children were even killed there. (Yes, that was a frequently repeated allegation.)
>
> Even the introduction of the word "hoax" was carefully calculated and with the mass media reporting that "conspiracy theorists" were using that term to describe the tragedy, many in the general public began to doubt the sanity of a lot of good people who were rightfully raising questions about what happened at Sandy Hook and the way that it was being exploited. (p. 289).

Taking Piper's analysis at face value, we might then view the trial of Alex Jones (who rightly or wrongly became the figurehead of "extremism" and "conspiratorialism" due to his own coverage of the Sandy Hook affair, which, it must be said, appeared on occasion to meet Piper's description of many so-called "truther" outlets) as the culmination of a "Deep State" program directed against promulgators of conspiratorial speech. At the time (and perhaps even still now), the trial appeared to have been the final nail in the conspiratorial coffin. Whether or not this was so, the public (and financial) humiliation of Alex Jones proved a significant feather in the cap of Cass Sunstein and his allies.

While the reaction to the Sandy Hook shooting and Boston Marathon bombing demonstrated by media, law enforcement, and the judicial system may not have been coordinated or mediated by Sunstein's strategy of conspiratorial suppression (as Piper suggests), Cass Sunstein nevertheless articulated the case for direct state intervention upon centers of conspiratorial discourse (as well as the methodologies to be used to that end) in the essay he co-authored with Adrian Vermeule. Of this plan, Piper says:

> Sunstein's insidious and Orwellian "think piece" began by raising this question: "Should governmental responses be addressed to the suppliers [of conspiracy theories] with a view to persuading or silencing them, or rather be addressed to the mass audience, with a view to inoculating them from pernicious theories?"
>
> While noting that, in his view, "these two strategies are not mutually exclusive," Sunstein went on to suggest that "perhaps the best approach is to straddle the two audiences with a single response or simply to provide multiple responses". However, Sunstein said, many officials considered it "an exercise in futility" to try to respond directly to "the suppliers of conspiracy theories" and that, instead, they tried to "address their responses to the third-party mass audience, hoping to stem the spread of conspiracy theories by dampening the demand rather than by reducing the supply."
>
> In answer to his own question "What can the government do about conspiracy theories?" Sunstein provided five possibilities:
>
> 1. Government might ban "conspiracy theories," somehow defined.
> 2. Government might impose some kind of tax, financial or otherwise, on those who disseminate such theories.
> 3. Government might itself engage in counterspeech, marshaling arguments to discredit conspiracy theories.
> 4. Government might formally hire credible private parties to engage in counterspeech.
> 5. Government might engage in informal communica-

> tion with such parties, encouraging them to help.
>
> Noting that each of these proposals had "a distinct set of potential effects, or costs and benefits, and each [of which] will have a place under imaginable conditions," Sunstein answered the specific question of "What should government do?" by stating quite directly: "Our main policy claim here is that government should engage in cognitive infiltration of the groups that produce conspiracy theories, which involves a mix of [the aforementioned proposals:] (3), (4), and (5)". (p. 283).

Will we ever have direct and incontrovertible proof linking responsible individuals, parties, and/or institutions to Sunstein, demonstrating irrefutably that such programs did exist, are still operational today, and are intended to militate against us? Likely the answer is no, or at least, not any time soon. Such is the nature of suspicion-culture, which seemingly by design relies on large aggregations of technical knowledge and historical learning to provide the bedrock for associative and intuitive leaps to be made which connect theory to actor(s), actor(s) to institution(s), and institution(s) to intention(s). What is incontrovertible, however, is the fact that not only are the institutions in place to manipulate folk discourse, but so is the willingness to do so. Of this, Piper says:

> Working from this standpoint Sunstein outlined what he called "a distinctive tactic for breaking up the hard core of extremists who supply conspiracy theories. "This program", he said, "involved the following: [C] ognitive infiltration of extremist groups, whereby government agents or their allies (acting either virtually or in real space, and either openly or anonymously) will undermine the crippled epistemology of believers by planting doubts about the theories and stylized facts that circulate within such groups, thereby introducing beneficial cognitive diversity".
>
> Because, Sunstein said, "conspiracy theorists are likely to approach evidence and arguments in a biased

way, they are not likely to respond well, or even logically, to the claims of [people they know to be] public officials," it was vital that, as Sunstein said, "government officials would participate anonymously or even with false identities" in 9-11 discussion groups and other conspiracy-focused gatherings on the Internet and elsewhere.

And with the increasingly widespread knowledge we now have about the capacity of the National Security Agency—among many government intelligence agencies in the United States alone—to monitor the telephone calls, emails, and other Internet activity of all Americans, we can certainly say, with utmost authority, that Sunstein and his co-conspirators and like-minded intriguers had already concluded that the framework was in place to be able to see precisely who was engaged in conspiracy talk and with whom they were communicating.

It is thus no coincidence that when the series of scandals erupted over the summer of 2013 regarding the activities of the National Security Agency (NSA) that Cass Sunstein was one of the four members of the so-called "independent" panel appointed by President Barack Obama charged with the responsibility of "reviewing" the operations of the NSA and other government agencies. And nor, we might add, it is any coincidence that another member of the panel, Richard Clarke (a former high-ranking advisor to presidents—Democratic and Republican alike—in the realm of "national security") now happens to head a private firm known as Good Harbor Security Risk Management. And yes, as you might have guessed, Good Harbor touts "Crisis Management" as one of its specialties. Crisis Management—that's what it's all about".(p. 284).

So not only does the regime *generate* suspicion-culture, but it also actively *participates* in that culture with the aims of distorting and impairing it. We know now that the state—through the various extensions of power-knowledge —is able and willing to apply pressure to dissipate or otherwise castrate dissent. While Cass is far from the only suspicion-architect worthy of identifying by name, through him we not only secure an important understanding of the campaign against misinformation/disinformation (a set of categorizations which we will soon be fixing our eyes upon) *but also* a peculiar element of suspicion-architecture: *the element of identity.* It is still not yet time for us to descend into these matters; I have only introduced this theme as a means for discussing the incestuousness of regime suspicion-culture, and to highlight the lengths it will go to in order to preserve itself. Come the third chapter, we will be better positioned to examine the origins of the open society, and of suspicion-culture more broadly. For now, we will set them aside in favor of the conspiratorial man himself.

CHAPTER TWO

The Measure of a (Conspiratorial) Man

A Science of the American Conspiracy Theorist

Over the course of the last seventy or so years, we have seen many attempts to understand what we are here calling *"suspicion-culture"*, and with those attempts came explanations for and accounts of the suspicion-possessed man himself. I will delay further discussion of the former until the close of this chapter in favor of the latter, which is of more immediate concern to us anyway. In this chapter I will provide an account of the suspicious man from the perspective of the present contemporary neoliberal scientific consensus (as well as counterpoints from our own).

According to a 2017 study published in *Current Directions in Psychological Science* authored by Douglas, Sutton, and Cichoka, beliefs in conspiracy theories *"promise to satisfy important social psychological motives that can be characterized as epistemic (e.g., the desire for understanding, accuracy, and subjective certainty), existential (e.g., the desire for control and security), and social (e.g., the desire to maintain a positive image of the self or group)"*.[1] As regards epistemic motives they note

1 Karen M. Douglas, Robbie M. Sutton, and Aleksandra Cichocka. "The Psychology of Conspiracy Theories." *Current Directions in Psychological Science* 26, no. 6 (2017): 538–42.

that, "*...[C]onspiracy theories appear to provide broad, internally consistent explanations that allow people to preserve beliefs in the face of uncertainty and contradiction*", are "*stronger among people who habitually seek meaning and patterns in the environment, including believers in paranormal phenomena*", as well as when "*events are especially large in scale or significant and leave people dissatisfied with mundane, small-scale explanations*". According to Douglas and her team, while adherence to conspiracy theories satisfies the need for "*cognitive closure*", particularly for individuals experiencing "*distress as a result of feeling uncertain*", it is often the case that such attempts "*may be more appealing than satisfying*" as the team's analysis suggests that "*conspiracy theories may satisfy some epistemic motives at the expense of others—for example, by shielding beliefs from uncertainty while being less likely to be accurate*".

Of the second category, the existential motive, Douglas' team demonstrate its empirical legitimacy while lamenting the absence of proof to its efficacy. Citing Grzesiak-Feldman (2013)[2], Abalakina-Paap, Stephan, Craig, & Gregory (1999)[3], Bruder et al. (2013)[4], and van Prooijen & Acker (2015)[5], they show that "*people are likely to turn to conspiracy theories when they are anxious*", "*feel powerless*", or otherwise experience a "*lack of sociopolitical control or lack of psychological empower-*

2 Grzesiak-Feldman, Monika. "The effect of high-anxiety situations on conspiracy thinking." *Current Psychology* 32 (2013): 100-118.

3 Abalakina-Paap, Marina, Walter G. Stephan, Traci Craig, and W. Larry Gregory. "Beliefs in conspiracies." *Political Psychology* 20, no. 3 (1999): 637-647.

4 Bruder, Martin, Peter Haffke, Nick Neave, Nina Nouripanah, and Roland Imhoff. "Measuring individual differences in generic beliefs in conspiracy theories across cultures: Conspiracy Mentality Questionnaire." *Frontiers in psychology* 4 (2013): 225.

5 Van Prooijen, Jan-Willem, and Michele Acker. "The influence of control on belief in conspiracy theories: Conceptual and applied extensions." *Applied Cognitive Psychology* 29, no. 5 (2015): 753-761.

ment", and furthermore, that belief in conspiracy theories is reduced when "*their sense of control is affirmed*".

Lastly, of the social motive, the team find themselves in agreement with Cichocka, Marchlewska, & Golec de Zavala (2016)[6] when they remark that individuals entertain conspiracy theories as a defense against threats to their in-group (or its self-image). Socially motivated "conspiracy theorizing" occurs, according to the study, under the following circumstances,

1. Ostracism or persecution (driving the individual or group to defensively narrativize their experience).
2. Disadvantagedness (e.g., low status derived from ethnic or economic identity).
3. Loss (specifically the loss experienced by a political candidate; the demographic or constituency represented by that candidate may resort to conspiracy theorizing in the aftermath of their defeat).
4. Or as a general strategy of self-narrativizing in the face of an insurmountable force or rival.

Interestingly, the team identifies narcissism as a contributing factor to the development and adoption of conspiratorial modes of thought. To quote from the study here,

> [F]indings suggest that conspiracy theories may be recruited defensively, to relieve the self or in-group from a sense of culpability for their disadvantaged position. In keeping with this defensive motivation, conspiracy belief is associated with narcissism—an inflated view of oneself that requires external validation and is linked

6 Cichocka, Aleksandra, Marta Marchlewska, Agnieszka Golec de Zavala, and Mateusz Olechowski. "'They will not control us': Ingroup positivity and belief in intergroup conspiracies." *British journal of psychology* 107, no. 3 (2016): 556-576.

> to paranoid ideation (Cichocka, Marchlewska, & Golec de Zavala, 2016). Conspiracy belief is also predicted by collective narcissism—a belief in the in-group's greatness paired with a belief that other people do not appreciate it enough (Cichocka, Marchlewska, Golec de Zavala, & Olechowski, 2016).[7] Groups who feel that they have been victimized are more likely to endorse conspiracy theories about powerful out-groups (Bilewicz, Winiewski, Kofta, & Wójcik, 2013)[8].

As was the case for the previously cited motives, Karen Douglas and her team do not view the adoption of conspiratorial cognition as successful in satisfying the individual (or group's) needs. Quoting once more from the study, "*A feature of conspiracy theories is their negative, distrustful representation of other people and groups. Thus, it is plausible that they are not only a symptom but also a cause of the feelings of alienation and anomie—a feeling of personal unrest and lack of understanding of the social world—with which they are correlated*". (p. 540).

We will return to our examination of the literature on conspiracy theorists, but it is important to pause here, for a moment, and offer a few quick retorts. Douglas and her team eventually acknowledge the historical facticity of conspiracy, and in general, the thrust of their inquiry is to determine the extent to which adoption of conspiratorial views truly meets the psychological needs of the person undertaking them. However, in their conclusion they also discuss the need for understanding the "*consequences of conspiracy beliefs*" on "*vulnerable and disadvantaged populations*".(p. 541). We will

7 Cichocka, Aleksandra, Marta Marchlewska, and Agnieszka Golec De Zavala. "Does self-love or self-hate predict conspiracy beliefs? Narcissism, self-esteem, and the endorsement of conspiracy theories." *Social Psychological and Personality Science* 7, no. 2 (2016): 157-166.

8 Bilewicz, Michal, Mikołaj Winiewski, Mirosław Kofta, and Adrian Wójcik. "Harmful Ideas, The Structure and Consequences of Anti-S emitic Beliefs in P oland." *Political Psychology* 34, no. 6 (2013): 821-839.

see more of the latter (and less of the former) as we make our way deeper into the discussion for the simple reason that most academic research on the matter is deeply, fatally biased. Due to researchers' cynical commitment to neoliberal axioms, today's academy cannot deliver a truly substantive analysis of conspiratorialism. Even normative accounts of conspiratorial ideation—such as the one provided above—will ultimately be tainted by the social scientist's role as enforcer of state ideology.

Over the course of the last decade, researchers (with the immediate aftermath of COVID-19 really driving this line of inquiry) have more singularly focused on the decentralizing, detribalizing, and demystifying effects of information in our hot, hypermodern age. While the problem of paranoia has always been a thorn in America's side, in today's world the conjectures of conspiracy theorists are *a threat to our democracy.* I say these things not to besmirch or belittle the researchers' motives, rather, to highlight how obsequiously it is that contemporary inquiries into suspicion are carried out according to the preferences and priorities of the therapeutic state. The dual disciplinary cultures of science and medicine intervene, as only they can, *"attending"* to the *"disease"*, the *"problem"*, of so-called *"disinformation"*. The answer of course, rather *their* answer, is simple: *more.* More expertise, more faith in institutions, and more faith in reason. More solutions from experts who, themselves recognizing a pattern of duplicity and malfeasance demonstrated by the American government, nevertheless insist on psychologizing challenges to authority (an authority recognized by most to be illegitimate). The course chartered by the international technocratic order is not slated to change and so necessarily man's psychology must be accommodated to it. His emotions and thoughts, then, become of primary importance; in hypermodern America, suspicion is a personal matter to be understood exclusively in terms of the individual's habit of consumption, self-narrativization, and ultimately their life history. Implicit to their line of inquiry is the demand to *not* doubt, for their true goal (in most instances, at least) is to restore the cult of consensus. In some instances, it should be noted, the motivations of anti-disinformation experts are much more particular and foreboding. Now is not the time for *that* discussion however, so let us now turn our attention to the *traits* and *characteristics* of conspiracy theorists, having already explored some motivations for their doubting. That is, let us examine their traits and characteristics *according to today's scientific consensus.*

In the April 2018 edition of the journal *Personality and Individual Differences*, Ricky Green and Karen Douglas tested whether conspiratorialism had its roots in the attachment styles of infancy and early childhood.[9] As the pair argued:

> Recent theorizing in social psychology suggests that individuals use conspiracy theories as an attempted defensive mechanism to address psychological needs, including the existential need for security and control. Individuals with anxious attachment are preoccupied with their security, tend to hold a negative view of outgroups, are more sensitive to threats, and tend to exaggerate the seriousness of such threats. Secure and avoidant attachment styles, on the other hand, are less sensitive to threats and do not exaggerate such threats. Anxious attachment—compared to secure and avoidant attachment—could therefore potentially be a key predictor of conspiracy belief (p. 32). While controlling the factors typically associated with conspiratorialism (e.g., RWA, interpersonal trust, etc.), Green and Douglas were able to demonstrate that individuals higher in anxious attachment showed a greater tendency to believe in conspiracy theories.[10] Appeals to attachment

9 Ricky Green & Karen M. Douglas (2018), "Anxious attachment and belief in conspiracy theories", *Personality and Individual Differences*, vol. 125, pp. 30–37.

10 Attachment theory, the product of British psychoanalyst John Bowlby, argues that prolonged bouts of separation from the mother result in

> theory vary, however, as differing teams have found evidence for the influence of avoidant attachment style on conspiratorialideation.[11] Moreover, the quality of a child's parental attachment is not wholly determined at the individual or familial level, for it is predicated on larger and more complex domains of human organization. The structure and stability of the family unit is greatly determined by economic, geographical, historical, and political factors, many of which individuals and families find themselves reacting to, not directing. While as a point of fact emotionally disrupted children are more likely to doubt those around them, any society which generates the anti-social conditions which disrupt family formation and maintenance surely must take a greater share of the responsibility for the matter. In fact, a recent study demonstrated *"a 15 percent decrease in secure attachment, along with a 56 percent spike in dismissive attachment and a nearly 18 percent increase in the fearful style—the two types associated with lack of trust and self-isolation"*.[12] Trends such as these place all relevant phenomena downstream of broader macropolitical developments.

Another study published in 2018, this time appearing in the *Journal of Individual Differences*, concluded that conspiratorial ideation was not dependent on mortality salience (an

measurable, long-term consequences for infant development and overall well-being. The "anxiously attached child" (or ambivalently attached) is one who experienced erratic or otherwise unpredictable caregiving, and thus lapses into anger or helplessness. As an adult, they will experience a great deal of interpersonal conflict (among other markers of psychological and social distress).

11 Luigi Leone, Mauro Giacomantonio, Riccardo Williams, Desiree Michetti (2018). "Avoidant attachment style and conspiracy ideation", *Personality and Individual Differences*, vol. 134, pp. 329–336.

12 Hill, Faith. 2023. "America Is In Its Insecure-Attachment Era." *The Atlantic*, April 27, 2023. https://www.theatlantic.com/family/archive/2023/04/insecure-attachment-style-intimacy-decline-isolation/673867/.

individual's sensitivity to or awareness of death) or feelings of powerlessness alone, but more specifically on the possession of traits indicating a form of schizotypy.[13] Now, schizotypy is both a theoretical concept and a continuum of traits and characteristics rather than a discrete cognitive state or medical condition. We ought to understand the behavior of individuals who demonstrate these characteristics as being "within arm's reach" of something like a schizophrenic (or otherwise psychotic) episode. Some are more at risk than others and no two may look the same in their presentation, but all the same, they participate in a "personality style" prone to delusion. Schizotypy is observable in the individual's predisposition for atypical cognitive and perceptual experiences (such as delusions or hallucinations), his disordered cognition, his introversion and anhedonia (more evidence for our "joylessness hypothesis"), and lastly his impulsivity and his nonconformity.[14] [15] Returning to the study proper, Hart and Grather (the authors of the study) identify conspiracy believers as *"individuals who are relatively untrusting, ideologically eccentric, concerned about personal safety, and prone to perceiving agency in actions and profundity in bullshit"* and, in a sample size of over 1,200 participants, attribute the acceptance of non-partisan conspiracy theories to a condition of schizotypy which gives rise to these characteristics. One problem with this explanation (at least, it is a problem for those of us who would like to say more about the general population based on such findings), is that it does not help us understand the broader phenomenon of suspicion-culture

13 Joshua Hart and Molly Grather. "Something's Going on Here." *Journal of Individual Differences*, vol. 39, no.4, Oct. 2018, pp. 229–237.

14 Bentall, R.P., Claridge, G. and Slade, P.D. (1989). The multi-dimensional nature of schizotypal traits: a factor analytic study with normal subjects. *British Journal of Clinical Psychology*, 28, 363–375.

15 Claridge, G., McCreery, C., Mason, O., Bentall, R., Boyle, G., Slade, P., & Popplewell, D. (1996). The factor structure of 'schizotypal' traits: A large replication study. *British Journal of Clinical Psychology*, 35, 103–115.

given that schizotypy—as a concept—is itself uncertain of its own general applicability.[16] It does confirm a stereotype (from the point of view of essentialism) of the conspiratorial person, and so at the least the *image* of the conspiratorial man persists.

However, other attempts to essentialize conspiratorialism have been less successful (usually the result of some failure at the conceptual level). A 2013 study published in *Frontiers in Psychology* demonstrated just this when a team of researchers found that in almost all cases, correlations between conspiracist ideation and FFM (Five-Factor Model) personality traits were "small and somewhat unstable".[17] Some teams have been able to link conspiratorial ideation to aspects of our personality (largely through self-reports and other questionnaires), for example: high extroversion and low agreeableness,[18] low conscientiousness and low openness to change,[19] high psychoticism,[20] to name a few. That conspiratorial ideation is routinely correlated with a wide range of "negative" person-

16 Tomohisa Asai, Eriko Sugimori, Naoko Bando, Yoshihiko Tanno, (2011). "The hierarchic structure in schizotypy and the five-factor model of personality", *Psychiatry Research*, vol. 185, Issues 1–2, pp. 78–83,

17 Robert Brotherton, Christopher C. French, and Alan D. Pickering, (2013). "Measuring belief in conspiracy theories: the generic conspiracist beliefs scale", *Frontiers in Psychology*, vol. 4, pp. 1–15.

18 Gonçalves, André, Gabriel Franco, Gabriel Vitor Gomes, Gisele Machado, Giselle Pianowski, and Lucas de Francisco Carvalho. 2022. "Personality and Adherence to the COVID-19 Vaccine: The Role of Agreeableness and Openness Traits." *Archives of Psychiatry and Psychotherapy* 24 (1): 13–21.

19 Rezende, Alessandro Teixeira, Valdiney Veloso Gouveia, Ana Karla Silva Soares, and Heloísa Bárbara Cunha Moizéis. 2021. "Crenças Em Teorias Da Conspiração Em Estudantes Universitários: Uma Explicação a Partir Dos Traços de Personalidade." *Psicología Conocimiento y Sociedad* 11 (2): 84–98

20 Blaauw, Elien M. n.d. "The Association between Maladaptive Personality Traits and Belief in Conspiracy Theories." Uvt.Nl. Accessed August 10, 2023.

ality traits (particularly in the context of a post-pandemic world, where compliance and conformity are integral to the neoliberal order), also raises certain "meta" level questions about psychometry in general, demonstrating how beholden to the political consensus researchers of today's academy are. It may yet be possible to discover the exact personality substrate which impels conspiratorial ideation, but this will not be done by the present generation of "consensus" researchers.

While endeavors to unequivocally excavate the origins of conspiratorialism from our deep personality have mostly failed, investigations into the relationship between cognitive style and conspiratorialism (as already noted elsewhere) have proven fruitful. Taken from a sample size of 508 individuals, Georgiou and his team demonstrated that people with ASD more strongly endorsed conspiracy theories than neurotypical people, concluding that traits associated with autism spectrum disorder mediated certain socio-cognitive factors including ambiguity tolerance, mindedness, and predisposition toward analytic or intuitive thinking in favor of conspiracy belief.[21] Neurodivergent types, on account of their unique state of being, are often less susceptible to the normative social forces which compel us to act or think in a certain way, and furthermore, are more prone to "eccentric" pursuits. While this explanation helps us to understand those persistent social undercurrents productive of conspiratorialism, it does not give us any insight into the phenomenon of a doubting mass society. Some, perhaps even many, conspiracy theorists are neurodivergent, but such individuals do not form the engine which drives suspicion-culture.

The research presented thus far presupposes that conspiratorial ideation is a private and individual phenomenon. But

21 Neophytos Georgiou, Paul H. Delfabbro, Ryan Balzan (2021). "Could autistic traits be a risk factor for conspiracy beliefs? An analysis of cognitive style and information seeking behavior.", *Minerva Psychiatry*, vol. 62, no. 4, pp. 231–240.

what if this tendency towards distrust were learned over time, an adaptation that aided us throughout our development? Assuming a non-pathological account puts us, then, on more conventional and evolutionary grounds of explanation. In a study published in 2019 by Raihiani and Bell, paranoia is placed on just such a footing.[22] Quoting from the study,

> Attempts to answer the question of why some people are more paranoid than others have typically appealed to proximate level explanations such as genetics, life history or cognitive biases. Nevertheless, these approaches do not answer the issue of why we have a cognitive capacity for paranoid thinking and whether between-individual variation in paranoid thinking might, in some environments, be selectively advantageous in fitness terms. From a Darwinian perspective, a fearful response to danger, whether actual or potential, is likely to carry significant fitness benefits and to have been subject to strong selection in many species. Nevertheless, not all individuals show an equivalent magnitude of response to the same threatening stimulus or context: levels of fearfulness differ markedly across individuals, even within a species. The question of how stable, between-individual differences in fearful responses might arise and be stabilised by selection falls under a broader banner of research on the evolution of stable behavioural types. Research in this field has shown that the evolution of variation in behavioural types stems from trade-offs in pursuing different fitness-relevant activities. For example, investing in growth (e.g. via foraging) often comes with an attendant increased risk of predation and so strategies aimed at increasing growth are likely to be traded-off against strategies that reduce predation risk. Organisms must therefore balance the rewards of investment in growth against the increased mortality risk; the optimal reso-

22 Raihani N.J., Bell V. (2019). "An evolutionary perspective on paranoia", *Nature Human Behavior,* vol. 3, pp. 114–121.

lution of such trade-offs in different environments or for different individuals can therefore select for variation in fearfulness, aggression, risk appetite and so on, which broadly dictate individual life history strategies and associated behaviour. (p. 116).

In addition to balancing such trade-offs, organisms must also effectively manage costs from errors that occur due to perceptual uncertainty ("error management theory"). Specifically, error management theory (also conceptualised as 'the smoke detector principle' in evolutionary medicine) predicts that when there are asymmetries in the costs of false-positive and false-negative error types, selection will favour strategies that minimise the chance of making the costlier error, even if this produces many behavioural mistakes. Following the logic of error management theory, previous evolutionary accounts have suggested that paranoia is an evolved psychological mechanism shaped by the selective pressures of catastrophic harm from others that is tuned to have a low threshold for detecting social threat. Individual variation in the relative asymmetry of error types is proposed to account for variation in paranoia across the full spectrum.

A coalitional perspective suggests that variation in paranoia could function to protect individuals from coalitionary threat in specific contexts and therefore serve an adaptive function when either the probability and/or the costs of harm from others are high. A prediction of this hypothesis is therefore that variation in paranoid thinking will reflect the background probability and/or costs of coalitional conflict. Epidemiological evidence supports this prediction: an increased tendency for paranoid thinking has been documented in general population groups that are involved in higher-than-average rates of coalitionary aggression, such as gang members and army veterans. The probability of inter-coalitionary violence is increased under conditions of resource scarcity and, as expected, living in poverty is also associated with increased tendency for

> paranoid thinking. (p. 117).

Richard Friedman, a psychiatrist, echoed this hypothesis in a 2021 publication of the journal *Psychiatric Services* when he said,

> Having the capacity to imagine and anticipate that other people might form coalitions and conspire to harm one's clan would confer a clear adaptive advantage: a suspicious stance toward others, even if mistaken, would be a safer strategy than carefree trust. The paranoia that drives individuals to constantly scan the world for danger and suspect the worst of others probably once provided a similar survival edge.[23]

The evolutionary account gives us a more robust understanding of suspicion-culture, one that is free of hostile and inconclusive pathologizing. In the accounts provided up to now, conspiratorial ideation ("paranoia") results from some essential dysfunction, or otherwise, dysfunctions of the individual and his specific ecological conditions. Here, "paranoia" is normative. Better still, it is advantageous, and so from this point of view we might begin to look at suspicion-culture more constructively as resulting from an external crisis (whether potential or actual). In its earlier formulation, the evolutionary account of life had a way of fortifying liberal presuppositions, giving the state the means by which it might more fully realize itself. Neoliberalism, however, breaks from the theoretical and even affective axioms of which it had developed from, giving evolutionist accounts an added reactionary edge, thereby making of it an opponent or adversary of 21st century state ideology. But is it a credible opponent?

As it turns out, the threat posed by evolutionist accounts is entirely in doubt. Today's evolutionist accounts of human cognition and conduct are phantastical attempts to escape neo-

23 Richard A. Friedman (2021). "Why Humans Are Vulnerable to Conspiracy Theories", *Psychiatric Services*, vol. 72, issue 1, p. 3–4.

liberal ontology; at the bottom of contemporary evolutionary lines of inquiry is the following meta-query: what would *x* be like if we humans weren't completely retarded? In taking up this discourse we wade from one form of mystification to another. Evolutionary explanations certainly provide us with a measure of plausibility *and for all we know they just might be true*. However, arguments delivered to us in this manner fail to provide the mechanism necessary to authorize them and without a mechanism, we cannot grant this argument its sacrosanctity (much less grant it its *scienticity*). And, as we have already noted, our contemporary neoliberal order could not even apply its own finding in service of itself, for to uphold the Darwinian dictum of adaptation would undermine the dual cults of expertise and consensus, potentially destabilizing the open society altogether. (Reasserting the dominance of these cults, of course, was the intention of the state's inquiry from the very beginning.) To "prove" the present-day incompatibility of suspicion would necessitate a kind of hair-splitting Darwinian pilpul that I do not believe American leadership is capable of mustering (to say nothing of whether such an effort would even succeed); all attempts to do so would require locating the precise moment or event where man's attitudes and methods of social organization were definitively transvaluated (a feat which cannot be achieved). Of course, we must doubt the importance of such a fact, even if its factuality could be satisfactorily demonstrated. From the point of view of social engineering and transhumanism, that suspicion was once advantageous to the species is hardly an obstacle to the utopic schemes of present-day leadership. Meddlers will do what comes naturally to them..

Returning to the theme of cynicism, and how "cynical reason" distorts scientific interpretation, let us consider the findings of a 2017 study published in the journal *Memory Studies*, which attributes the phenomenon of conspiratorial ideation to a generalized need for "*sense-making*", particularly during times of crisis.[24] However, even while admitting the fact of historical crises (as well as the fact of historical collusion), the researchers' role is as consensus-makers and gatekeepers of liberal hegemony and therefore a conspiracy is only as legitimate (or illegitimate) as the citations and sources that lead investigators van Prooijen and Douglas are encouraged to use.[25] To even attempt the arguments made in this study, van Prooijen and Douglas must participate in a phenomenon which has come to be known as cynical reason. Slavoj Zizek provided an excellent definition of this phenomenon when he declared that cynical reason is *"the feeling that we know very well that our present situation is invidious, but all the same we act as though it isn't"*.

24 van Prooijen, J.W., & Douglas, K. M. (2017). "Conspiracy theories as part of history: The role of societal crisis situations". *Memory Studies, 10* (3), 323–333.

25 Van Prooijen and Douglas employ the following definition of "societal crisis":

> *"Societal crises [are] impactful and rapid societal change that calls existing power structures, norms of conduct, or even the existence of specific people or groups into question. Since people have a fundamental need to understand why events occurred, particularly in the case of negative or unexpected events, crisis situations often elicit sense-making narratives among citizens that become part of their representations of history. Many of these narratives take the form of conspiracy theories, commonly defined as explanatory beliefs of how multiple actors meet in secret agreement in order to achieve a hidden goal that is widely considered to be unlawful or malevolent."*

Examples of illegitimate conspiracy theories, at least illegitimate in the view of Douglas and van Prooijen, include the CIA's involvement in both the JFK assassination and the 9/11 attacks:

> *"While some conspiracy theories have turned out to be true (e.g. the Watergate and Iran–Contra scandals), most conspiracy theories in history have no evidence to support them. Well-known examples of conspiracy theories as explanations of societal crises are allegations that the Central Intelligence Agency (CIA) was behind the assassination of President John Fitzgerald Kennedy (JFK) or that the Bush administration was involved in plotting the 9/11 terrorist attacks."*

To be a functionary of the neoliberal technocratic regime is to be a practitioner of cynical reason. Said differently (that is, without the veneer of philosophical restraint), one must be willing to practice deception (primarily, or at least initially, towards oneself) and perceive it as enlightenment. More will be said on this subject in the fourth chapter—as relates to both the meaning of and solution to cynical reason—but for now it is sufficient to recognize in cynical reason both the fulfillment of a classical Enlightenment mode of operating and a mutation, a progression or development, which has fundamentally impaired Man and damaged, perhaps irrevocably, his social ecology. We observe cynical reason at work in most spheres of human living, but it is the functionaries of the state who offer the most virtuosic demonstrations.

The duo argues that:

> If belief in conspiracy theories is a way of making sense of a situation, it follows that such beliefs are increasingly likely to the extent that people experience uncertainty or a lack of control. This assertion would provide an explanation for why conspiracy theories emerge in societal crisis situations: People often experience such situations as uncontrollable, and hence, they are a cause of substantial uncertainty and anxiety among citizens. Moreover, it is often easy to connect societal crises to the purposeful misdeeds of hostile groups, making it likely that many citizens consider the possibility of secret conspiracy formation. {p. 327).

Douglas and van Prooijen identify two problematic consequences of this tendency, the first being the asymmetry between one's adoption of and commitment to conspiracizing and the degree to which doing so genuinely ameliorates the distress they are experiencing. No attention is paid to the possibility of macropolitical factors causing distress and chaos, of course. The second consequence (and the more relevant one to van Prooijen and Douglas' roles as consensus-makers) is the problem of conspiracy theories growing into intergenerational representations of history. That is, the production and passing on of historical counter-narratives. To hear them frame it in their own words,

> [W]e propose that while conspiracy theories may originate through the emotional processes of lacking control or feeling uncertain, at a relatively fast pace they can become coherent narratives that shape people's representations of history (see also Hilton and Liu, this issue). The feature of conspiracy theories that they summarize complex events into a simplified story—typically involving a powerful enemy group (i.e. the conspiracy) that deliberately organizes and carries out an evil plan—makes such theories ideally suited for cultural transmission as they are easily understood by lay people. It has been noted that people typically make sense of past events as "lay historians" who—unlike professional historians—rarely base their conclusions on direct historical sources. Instead, lay historians transmit historical narratives to others based on their imperfect memory, as well as on other imperfect sources of information such as folklore, novels, films, and the like. (p. 329).

Folk accounts of history are an affront to the cult of expertise. To be clear, I am not participating in anti-intellectual polemics: I am remarking on the fact that the cult of expertise has collapsed, and consistent with a degenerate totalitarian political order, it is not interested in turning inwards for solutions but rather continuing to harangue, manipulate, and extort the governed into a state of penitence (and thus, back into submission). Interestingly, the researchers lament certain facts which undermine their "irrationalist hypothesis" of conspiracizing. Van Prooijen and Douglas observe that conspiratorialism surrounding the JFK assassination has only *increased* in the sixty years since it occurred, demonstrating that fear and uncertainty are not the only factors (perhaps, *not even the most significant factors*) in the development and promulgation of conspiratorialism. This only vindicates the need for a folk account of history, especially when we consider the state's unwillingness to fully disclose the truth of contentious historical events.

The irrationalist hypothesis of conspiratorialism remains strong, however, with many adherents (as well as many expressions). Roland Imhoff and Martin Bruder wrote (in a study published in the *European Journal of Personality*) that conspiratorialism is best understood as a generalized political attitude or mentality—one that is distinct from RWA and SDO (right-wing authoritarianism and social dominance orientation).[26] According to their findings, conspiratorialism is more closely related to prejudice against high-power groups that are perceived as both less likeable and more threatening than low-power groups. Oliver and Wood echo this finding, at least partially, when they declare conspiratorialism as distinct from conservatism and authoritarianism. For them it is much closer to what Richard Hofstadter infamously termed "the paranoid style" in its predisposition for naïve Manichaeism.[27] This view gives the "conspiracy theory" a kind of systemic, ideological weight, and as such treats it less frivolously. A recent study from the "Psychopathology" section of the journal *Frontiers in Psychology* drew much the same conclusion.[28] Citing the work of philosopher Quassim Cassam, Martinez and his team of

26 Imhoff, Roland, and Martin Bruder. "Speaking (Un-)Truth to Power: Conspiracy Mentality as a Generalised Political Attitude." *European Journal of Personality 28*, no. 1 (2013): 25-43.

27 Oliver, J E., and Thomas J. Wood. "Conspiracy Theories and the Paranoid Style(S) of Mass Opinion." *American Journal of Political Science 58*, no. 4 (2014): 952–966.

28 Martinez, Anton P., Shevlin, Mark, Valiente, Carmen, Hyland, Philip, and Richard P. Bentall. "Paranoid Beliefs and Conspiracy Mentality Are Associated with Different Forms of Mistrust: A Three-nation Study." *Frontiers in Psychology 13*, (2022): 1–11.

investigators argued that,

> Although the authors of these articles do not regard conspiracy theories as a reflection of an underlying psychopathology, they consider that certain psychopathological traits might facilitate the belief in conspiracy theories. Contrary to this view, authors such as the philosopher [Cassam] argue that studying conspiracy theories from an individual differences perspective fails to address one of the most important features of these theories, which is that they are often politically motivated. From this perspective, conspiracy theories can be thought of as ideologies (i.e., set of ideas and beliefs) that structure the understanding of the political world, and thus considering them as a trait of an underlying psychopathology underestimates the social harm that can cause. In future research, it would be useful to compare how paranoia and conspiracy theories relate to political psychology variables, for example authoritarianism, collective mistrust, mistrust to specific outgroups, mistrust to political figures and authorities, which we anticipate would be associated with the latter and not the former. (p. 6).

Their work is an improvement, at least in the sense of taking a normative view of the matter, which sadly does not take us as far as we need to go (assuming a genuine understanding of suspicion-culture is what we are all, in fact, pursuing). The social scientist, as a functionary of the state and a practitioner of cynical reason, may adopt a broader and more holistic framework but he or she only does so to better execute the demands of the state. "Conspiracy theorizing" as the ideology of our "dormant dissident" is certainly a more accurate assessment than we have yet seen, though such a picture is hardly complete. More than just presenting conspiratorialism as irrational (e.g., prejudicial, adversarial), the findings just discussed paint a rather Schmittian view of conspiracy theorists. They don't just engage in suspicious conjectures about people-groups or classes they dislike, they organize an oppositional worldview to formalize their disdain for the powerful. Again, the question of why individuals or groups might come to malign the powerful and well-situated is virtually *never* meaningfully engaged with by researchers of conspiratorialism.

Some researchers have provided demographic accounts of the conspiracy theorist and to that we shall now turn our attention. Karen Douglas (a name now familiar to us) provides a brief overview of the demographic literature concerning conspiratorialism, beginning first with the link to education.[29] Citing Uscinski and Parent (2014), conspiracy theorists are less well educated with lower incomes, and as per the findings of Freeman and Bentall (2017), they are more likely to be unmarried and/or unemployed men (while earlier research pointed to a greater susceptibility among women, some researchers have shown that this is true with respect to *paranormal beliefs* rather than politically conspiratorial ones). At least one study implicates religiosity as a predictor for conspiratorial ideation.[30] Status as an ethnic minority is also indicative of conspiratorial thinking (some studies show African and Hispanic Americans to be more conspiratorially minded on average than ethnically White Americans, though the image portrayed by popular

29 Douglas, Karen M., Uscinski, Joseph E., Sutton, Robbie M., Cichocka, Aleksandra, Nefes, Turkay, Ang, Chee Siang, and Farzin Deravi. "Understanding Conspiracy Theories." *Advances in Political Psychology 40*, no. S1 (2022): 3–35.

30 Lucas Stasielowicz (2022). "Who believes in conspiracy theories? A meta-analysis on personality correlates", *Journal of Research in Personality*, vol. 98.

culture muddles this rather considerably).[31] [32] [33] Interestingly, conspiratorial sentiment is lowest among those working in finance, the military, and the government.[34] (We need not ponder long the possible explanations for *that* data set.) A study of elected officials in Louisiana (all African American), found conspiratorialism to be as widespread among "elites" as it is among the "masses" (a fact which doubtless complicates the image of conspiratorialism presented by the technocratic neoliberal regime). Politically speaking, Douglas' analysis finds support for the infamous "horseshoe theory" of political organization; citing van Prooijen, Krouwel, and Pollet (2015), in both the United States as well as the Netherlands, conspiratorialism is common among those situated on the "far-left" and "far-right" of the political spectrum.[35] According to Uscinski, Klofstad, and Atkinson (2016), however, conspiratorialism is more commonly observed among self-identified independents and those affiliated with some third party.[36] Even though some research has concluded that conspiratorialism is closer

31 Ted Goertzel (1994), "Belief in Conspiracy Theories", *Political Psychology*, vol. 15, no. 4, pp. 731–742.

32 Sharon Parsons, William Simmons, Frankie Shinhoster, John Kilburn, (1999). "A test of the grapevine: An empirical examination of conspiracy theories among African Americans", *Sociological Spectrum*, vol. 19, issue 2, pp. 201–222.

33 Crocker, J., Luhtanen, R., Broadnax, S., & Blaine, B. E. (1999). Belief in U.S. Government Conspiracies Against Blacks among Black and White College Students: Powerlessness or System Blame? *Personality and Social Psychology Bulletin*, 25(8), 941–953.

34 Uscinski, J. E., & Parent, J. M. (2014). *American conspiracy theories*. New York, NY: Oxford University Press.

35 van Prooijen, J.-W., Krouwel, A. P. M., & Pollet, T. (2015). Political extremism predicts belief in conspiracy theories. *Social Psychological and Personality Science*, 6(5), 570–578.

36 Uscinski, J. E., Klofstad, C., & Atkinson, M. D. (2016). What drives conspiratorial beliefs? The role of informational cues and predispositions. *Political Research Quarterly*, 69(1), 57–71.

to an affect than a psychopathology or heritable trait, Douglas' review emphasizes the link between conservatism and conspiratorialism.[37] [38] While we have already discussed findings to the contrary, nonetheless Douglas cites numerous studies highlighting the relationship between conspiratorialism and, for brevity's sake, other well-known right-wing signifiers.[39] [40] [41] To account for some of the conclusions drawn by academics studying conspiratorialism, Douglas does offer the following caveat:

> [I]t may simply be the case that the bulk of the research has been conducted by left-leaning researchers. There have been many studies of conspiracy theories held by the right (going back to Hofstadter, 1964), but few studies focusing on conspiracy theories held by the left. The end result is that researchers may overlook conspiracy theories closer to home. (p. 12).

There remains one obvious demographic we have neglected thus far (the inclusion of which would greatly aid our understanding of conspiratorialism): *losers.* On this point, Douglas says the following:

37 Galliford, N., & Furnham, A. (2017). Individual difference factors and beliefs in medical and political conspiracy theories. *Scandinavian Journal of Psychology*, 58, 422–428.

38 Miller, J. M., Saunders, K. L., & Farhart, C. E. (2016). Conspiracy endorsement as motivated reasoning: The moderating roles of political knowledge and trust. *American Journal of Political Science*, 60(4), 824–844.

39 Bruder, M., Haffke, P., Neave, N., Nouripanah, N., & Imhoff, R. (2013). Measuring individual differences in generic beliefs in conspiracy theories across cultures: Conspiracy mentality questionnaire. *Frontiers in Psychology*, 4(225).

40 Grzesiak-Feldman, M., & Irzycka, M. (2009). Right-wing authoritarianism and conspiracy thinking in a Polish sample. *Psychological Reports*, 105(2), 389–393.

41 Richey, S. (2017). A birther and a truther: The influence of the authoritarian personality on conspiracy beliefs. *Politics & Policy*, 45(3), 465–485.

Situational factors, such as being on the losing end of a power asymmetry, could lead to increased belief in conspiracy theories. Uscinski and Parent argue that conspiracy theories are for "losers" and tend to accuse those in power and their coalitions. Examining letters to the editor of the New York Times spanning 1890–2010, they found that when a Republican was president, the resonant conspiracy theories tended to accuse Republicans and big business of conspiring, but when a Democrat was in office, the conspiracy theories tended to accuse Democrats and socialists of conspiring. They also found that during declared wars and the Cold War conspiracy theories focused on foreign enemies more than during other times. Edelson et al found that electoral losers were more likely than winners to believe that fraud had occurred. (p. 12).

One assumption of the "losers" idea is that conspiracy theories communicate information to generate collective action in the face of threat. To test this, Smallpage et al. asked an Mturk sample in the United States to match a series of partisan and nonpartisan conspiracy theories to the party most associated with each one. They found that partisans—even those who did not believe in the conspiracy theories themselves—correctly matched which conspiracy theories were "owned" by which party. They concluded that conspiracy theories function like calling cards sending clear signals to copartisans. By doing this, conspiracy theories could generate collective action. With this said, more work needs to investigate the effect of conspiracy theories on collective political actions such as voting.

Also, research and theory on the relationship between political conviction and conspiracy belief is clear, and even settled, on some points but not on others. As we have seen, it is clear that people on both sides of the left-right political spectrum entertain conspiracy beliefs about the other side. However, some scholars maintain that conspiracy theories are more characteristic of the right than the left. Others dispute this and

> suggest that conspiracy theories are overwhelmingly bipartisan—found on both sides of any political debate. Still others find that conspiracy theories are stronger at the political extremes. A great deal more work involving comparative studies of conspiracy theories in different political epochs, of conspiracy theories in different contemporary polities, and different varieties of conspiracy belief, is required. (p. 13).

As far as normative accounts go, Douglas' findings are probably the least controversial. For many, especially where partisanship is concerned, cries of foul play are quite commonplace (and not likely to arouse sympathy). Of course, this account does not give us any insight into the legitimacy of such claims but then again, this is an investigation into *psychological* research, after all. By now I hope I have presented a diversity of investigations sufficient to dispel the belief that conspiratorialism is reducible to a single trait or demographic. If anything, at least from the perspective of regime narratives, there is no single net which can catch all conspiracy theorists at once (and this fact proves more and more troublesome for the regime every day). Legitimacy can only be won through unity; for all its strengths, neoliberal technocracy is increasingly defined by its *dis*unity and thus it can only further alienate (thus, in the process, furthering production of suspicion-culture).

Let us now give our attention to an account of conspiratorialism that *doesn't* originate from a social science department. After all, a phenomenon as curious and vexing as conspiratorialism is sure to catch the eye of investigators from all arenas of life. What psychologists refer to as "hyperactive agency detection", Reed Berkowitz simply calls "*guided apophenia*". German physician Klaus Conrad first coined the phrase *apophenia* in 1958 to explain the development of schizophrenia, whereas Reed drew from his decades of experience as a video game designer to attempt an explanation of the QAnon phenomenon.[42]

In QAnon, Berkowitz saw a sinister and Machiavellian "*Mirror Universe*" rendition of the spaces and environments he had spent his whole life creating.

"*When I saw QAnon, I knew exactly what it was and what it was doing. I had seen it before. I had almost built it before. It was gaming's evil twin. A game that plays people*", Berkowitz wrote.

In one of his first designing experiences, Berkowitz came to understand the phenomenon of apophenia; tasked with guiding his participants toward a specific set of clues, Reed thought he had idiot-proofed his construct (as it turns out, he was wrong). Players were routinely distracted by what they perceived as the "obvious" clues laid out before them.

> It was a problem because three of the pieces made the shape of a perfect arrow pointing right at a blank wall. It was uncanny. It had to be a clue. The investigators stopped and stared at the wall and were determined to figure out what the clue meant and they were not going one step further until they did. The whole game was derailed. Then, it got worse. Since there obviously was no clue there, the group decided the clue they were looking for was IN the wall. The collection of ordinary tools they found conveniently laying around seemed to enforce their conclusion that this was the correct direction. The arrow was pointing to the clue and the tools were how they would get to it. How obvious could it be?

Berkowitz argues that because there is a telos to the kinds of games professionals like him construct, because things are purposeful, the agency of the player can drive them to misinterpret or misapprehend the given facts. A certain hyperre-

42 Berkowitz, Reed. "A Game Designer's Analysis of QAnon: Playing with reality", Medium. September 30, 2020. https://medium.com/curioserinstitute/a-game-designers-analysis-of-qanon-580972548be5.

ality, in the sense invoked by Dutch linguist and philosopher of madness Wouter Kusters, emerges, such that the clues and meanings discovered by the players are *more* real than those constructed by the game developers (and thus *more* worthy of investigation, even when that investigation appears, at least initially, fruitless). QAnon, however, is an inversion of this scenario for there is, in fact, no point to the cryptic messages left behind by the then anonymous "Q".

> Here apophenia is the point of everything. There are no scripted plots. There are no puzzles to solve created by game designers. There are no solutions", Berkowitz observes, "QAnon grows on the wild misinterpretation of random data, presented in a suggestive fashion in a milieu designed to help the users come to the intended misunderstanding. Maybe "guided apophenia" is a better phrase. Guided because the puppet masters are directly involved in hinting about the desired conclusions. They have pre-seeded the conclusions. They are constantly getting the player lost by pointing out unrelated random events and creating a meaning for them that fits the propaganda message Q is delivering.

In other words, where we go one, we go all—into the proverbial Desert of the Real. The "guided apophenia" of conspiratorialism, that is if we take Berkowitz's account as correct, describes the very phenomenon—certainly from the point of view of the regime—which threatens to implode our very way of life. So-called "disinformation", whether we speak of rumors of alleged crisis actors at school shootings or the latest "Q drop", represents this guided apophenia, as pied pipers of the information hazard run roughshod across our democracy, wreaking havoc on our minds. Guided apophenia of this kind relies in large part on *pre*-suading the target of the validity of the information being presented. In the case of Q, that pre-suasion was secured through the cult of personality surrounding Donald Trump. Through the medium of Donald Trump, the message of QAnon would find safe passage. Of course, there is also a psychopolitical dimension heavily at play here; for the attempted pre-suasion to hold, there needed to be some psychic reserve (or desire) that the suspicion-architects behind QAnon could exploit. Thankfully for them, there was: a need for hope. Fox Mulder's dictum from *The X Files* ("*I want to believe*") was easily, evidently, on display for anyone with eyes to see and ears to hear. Tragically, though not surprisingly, it is only the folk account of history which "demands" an explanation, for it so often remains unsanctified, unauthorized, by any sovereign institution. When the state traffics in suspicion (which is to say, *cynicism*) the explanation as to why is always self-evident: for reasons of self-preservation. Never forget, either, that *dominance* is a form of self-preservation.

Not all examinations into the conspiracy theorist serve this exact function, and I would like to direct your attention to a sampling of conclusions *not* intended to buttress the state. Writing for the Italian journal "*Argumenta*", Kurtis Hagen expresses his concerns over the objectivity (or lack thereof) which social science researchers bring to bear on their studies of suspicion when he says,

> Many philosophers, including David Coady and Steve Clarke, have commented that academics have a "low opinion" of conspiracy theorists, or that conspiracy theorists are "unpopular amongst intellectuals". Indeed, it hardly takes a philosopher to notice that. But it is troubling to consider this in connection with the lopsided and unfair treatment of conspiracy theorists in the social science literature, for it suggests that these are not just "innocent mistakes" that could have gone either way. Rather, one must worry that bias against conspiracy theories is influencing the results of social science scholarship, with one biased finding building upon another. And while this article has been narrowly focused on the treatment of conspiracy theories in particular, it raises the question of the degree to which

> the social science literature more generally may be influenced by other widely shared biases.[43] (p. 324).

Hagen rejects the widespread (and widely accepted) notion of conspiratorialism as "monological", a view which claims that belief in one conspiracy engenders belief in other conspiratorial ideas. This assumption should concern us for, presuming its accuracy, it would mean that individuals imperil themselves by engaging in suspicion-discourse; in dipping their toes into the conspiracy pool, such individuals risk falling susceptible to an innumerable number of other conspiratorial ideations (the veracity of which, according to experts on the subject, are always to be doubted) by virtue of simply engaging with conspiratorialism in the first place! This implies a certain lack of rigor and agency on the part of the conspiracy theorist (which may be true), and when applied more broadly, analogizes conspiratorialism to a quicksand of the mind: the more you struggle to understand, the more you are trapped in a pit of suspicious ideation. Hagen's view rescues the rationality and agency of the conspiracy theorists, permitting of them executive level discriminatory powers.

The problem with the monological view, or so researchers of conspiratorialism would have us believe, is that this "monologism" drives conspiracy theorists to believe mutually exclusive accounts of history. Worst of all, their *"crippled epistemology"* (Sunstein and Vermeule's coinage) drives conspiracy theorists to believe wholly fictitious conspiracy theories. Hagen cites researchers like Sunstein and van Prooijan (both of whose findings we have already discussed at length) who use this claim to undermine and ridicule conspiratorial ideation by highlighting its seemingly obvious irrationality and inconsistency. Hagen quotes Swami et al., who argue that *"conspiracy beliefs form part of a 'monological belief system' in*

43 Kurtis Hagen, (2018). "Conspiracy Theorists and Monological Belief Systems", *Argumenta, vol.* 6, p. 303–324.

which a conspiratorial idea serves as evidence for other conspiracist ideation", and then proceeds to demonstrate the core problem of suspicion-skepticism as demonstrated by (neo) liberal consensus makers: their description of, shall we call it '*conspiratorial cognition*', is neither deserving of doubt nor condemnation. Of this Hagen says,

> However, there is something strange about pointing out this fact. For the reasoning it describes is both ubiquitous and epistemically unproblematic. Of course one belief serves as evidence for another, and so it should. There is hardly an alternative. (p. 315).

Belief that al Qaeda may have perpetrated the September 11 attacks based on a previously held belief in their role perpetrating other attacks (e.g., the U.S.S. Cole, embassy bombings in Africa) is eminently rational, Hagen argues, as *"the degree of credence one gives to one event is, and should be, influenced by one's beliefs about other events"*.

The author pushes his argument further when he challenges claims of "unrelatedness" in the belief system of conspiracy theorists. Setting aside the question of veracity, the simple fact of a man or woman believing a given authority ("The Authorities", even) to be *essentially* deceptive has good reason to entertain a variety of (seemingly) unrelated conspiracy theories, Hagen says. The question we must ask is on just what grounds are these "theories" unrelated? For Hagen, there remains no good reason to affirm their *epistemic* unrelatedness, particularly if we can demonstrate that belief in one event increases the probability of belief in other, different events. To do so is, in Hagen's words, "unproblematic". That researchers can identify the substrate of a given belief (or in this case, pattern of beliefs) can often prove remarkable, though considering Hagen's view, there is no reason to give such inordinate significance to accounts of conspiratorial ideation. It is only because such beliefs (were they contributions to an effectively organized political campaign), pose a threat to the *TIS* that a general phenomenon of cognition is misattributed to conspiratorial ideation (all in the vain hope that doing so will disempower folkish suspicion).

Hagen dispels other claims, such as the alleged closed-minded and anti-empirical nature of conspiracy theorists, citing Cass Sunstein himself to such effect (Sunstein has described conspiracy theorists as being *"spectacularly well-informed"*). In Hagen's view (a view which I endorse), the most problematic aspects of conspiratorial ideation as argued by some of their most prolific researchers (such as Ted Goertzel who Hagen specifically references, and whose research we have cited elsewhere) is that they struggle to demonstrate a factual basis for justifying their "odious" views. Crippled by their *"closed epistemology"*, conspiracy theorists never consult the material facts nor the social reality of their beliefs—at least, that is what neoliberal consensus makers would argue. Luminaries in the world of disinformation like Ted Goertzel and Cass Sunstein hurt their own cause by trying to make contradictory statements about conspiratorial ideation seem compatible (*"Their information is wrong"; "They don't attend to the facts"; "They don't debate their ideas"; "They are spectacularly well-informed"*), leaving other researchers like Karen Douglas and Robert Sutton to make sense of their inconsistencies. Hagen demonstrates this with painfully exacting reference to and citations of their work. He puts an excellent stamp on his rebuttal of conventional investigations into conspiratorial ideation when he argues that,

> After all, what would it take to prove that controversial conspiracy theories are implausible? Nothing less than addressing the relevant particulars directly—as well as sizing up all the prior probability factors. For the most part, academics shy away from this. Is it not conventionalist social scientists, then, who exhibit to a greater degree a problematic aspect of monological belief systems, in their relative unwillingness to engage

in debate, and to investigate the factual details? (p. 321).

Hagen finds nothing particularly interesting about the psychology of conspiracy theorists, suggesting that the actual cognitive factors at play are likely mundane and ubiquitous, explainable in terms of individual differences. Rather, Hagen suggests that investigations into "*conventionalists*" (as he calls them) would prove fruitful, if only for balancing out the field. Upon reaching his conclusion Hagen asked,

> For example, why did so many Americans believe that Saddam Hussein was in cahoots with al Qaeda? (We know that part of the reason is that officials actively encouraged this belief. The question is: Why did people buy it?) Relatedly, why did soldiers in Iraq believe they were avenging the victims of 9/11? Why did people believe the baby incubator story that was used to market the first Gulf War? Why do some people believe that Syrian President Bashar al-Assad would be so irrational as to use chemical weapons right after Obama declared that to do such a thing would be crossing a line that would ensure US military action against him (and almost did)—especially when the evidence presented was weak? (p. 323).

Each question would require its own line of investigation to answer, though I have proposed some general explanations so far here (and in previous works). Hagen has provided us with sound empirical reasons for doubting the "consensus" account of conspiratorial ideation but there remain others left to explore.

To round out this portion of the analysis, let us turn our attention at last to what we may term the "corruption theory" of conspiratorial ideation. Writing for the journal of *Social Psychology and Personality Science,* Sinan Alper and Roland Imhoff argue that the relevant factor in driving conspiratorial ideation is an *increased level of corruption.*[44] Taking up the position that CTs (conspiracy theories) function as a threat monitoring system (not unlike the evolutionary argument we discussed earlier in this chapter), belief in a given conspiracy theory, or even a general attitude of suspicion, would prove less costly to the individual than a failure in attending to such a possibility would. The "corruption theory" of conspiratorial ideation as presented by Alper and Imhoff adds much needed, and in fact illuminating, context to the claim (cited elsewhere in this chapter) that one's level of education influences his or her tendency towards conspiratorial ideation; countries with high levels of corruption provide the necessary "just cause" for conspiratorial ideation *regardless* of one's educational or class identity[45] (with "the West"—meaning North America, the United Kingdom, and Western Europe—ranking as "lower corruption countries" and "the Third World"—Africa, South America, Eastern Europe, the Mid and Far East—ranking among the highest). The Corruption Perceptions Index may dictate one thing, but if you, dear reader, doubt the United States' status as a "high corruption country" than I would simply remind you that only 1 of the last 6 Presidential elections passed without major, credible, claims of fraud and tampering. Digression aside, countries with higher levels of corruption saw partisanship increased (that is to say, conspiratorial ideation was directed, perspectivally, toward *"the usual suspects"*), so while skeptical ideations thrived, they did so in rigidly ideological ways. CTs on the political Left largely manifested as anti-business and anti-state, while CTs on the political Right were, broadly speaking, more nativistic in character.

44 Alper, S., & Imhoff, R. (2022). Suspecting Foul Play When It Is Objectively There: The Association of Political Orientation With General and Partisan Conspiracy Beliefs as a Function of Corruption Levels. *Social Psychological and Personality Science*, 0(0).

45 Alper, Sinan. 2021. "There Are Higher Levels of Conspiracy Beliefs in More Corrupt Countries." PsyArXiv. May 20.

Countries lower in corruption, however, saw conspiratorialism primarily on the Right, though with a curious detail: Right-wing practitioners of conspiratorial ideation in these "lower corruption countries" supported historically Left-wing conspiracy theories (e.g., big business, finance, government, et cetera). Liberal priors abound, thus rendering the authors' explanations for their findings convoluted and overwrought (and some of their methodological approaches flawed), though that by no means detracts from the value of their findings. They do comment on the possibility that, due to the Right's anti-elitist posture it may be amenable to more conventional Left-wing theories of a shadowy corporate elite. There are many reasons why such a development would occur, including: the facticity of many Left-wing CTs, the fact of the Left's abandonment of issues once considered to have been monopolized (anti-capitalism, for instance), the commodification of CTs themselves thereby leading to a greater cultural acceptance, and so on. Likely there are even more, perhaps *superior* explanations for this change in suspicion-culture. The exact details are of ultimately little import to the broader questions posed in this work. What is important, or at the least *useful*, are normative—that is, *non-pathological*—accounts of conspiratorialism such as those we have just concluded examining, for even in their flaws we learn something truer and more penetrating about suspicion-culture (and its production).

We began this discussion by examining the atomic, irrationalist, and pathological accounts of conspiratorial ideation before making our way to more conceptual, meaningfully empirical, and generally more rigorous accounts of the phenomenon. As we have already remarked, investigations into suspicion-culture suffer tremendously from the bias of those conducting them (and this has been a critical problem for the field ever since its earliest days); furthermore, such investigations serve a discrete, cynical function in that they aim to facilitate the consolidation and preservation of the *TIS*. I have given as thorough a review of the existing research as I can, all while offering concise rebuttals when necessary. A stronger account of conspiratorialism waits patiently, silently, in the wings. For now, it is less important to say something about the "state" or "condition" of those who engage in conspiratorial ideation than it is to take note of what those individuals and organizations, themselves being so troubled by the existence of dissenting thought, think to be true about the matter. Our aim is toward an understanding of the general phenomenon of suspicion-culture but also, more importantly, an understanding of its production. We study the findings of specialists in this area to better understand their processes and priorities, for in doing so, we position ourselves more effectively to rebuff them.

"Virtual shamanism" and Conspiratorialism as a Practice

Were we to take the findings provided to us by these "conventionalists" (better still, "consens-ists") straightforwardly we are still left with a very important question: do these conclusions help us better understand conspiratorial ideation? Moreover, do these findings aid us in understanding the suspiciously minded American man or woman? I think the answer, we must admit to ourselves, is *no*. *Even if* we cast aside the (modest) rebuttals discussed so far, we would still be forced to admit that the accounts provided by social scientists have all the weight and consistency of a plate of whipped cream. What, then, would provide us with a genuine and compassionate understanding of such individuals? If we truly wanted to *know* and to *connect* with conspiracy theorists—*to truly make contact with "the other", as good little Liberals*—how could such a thing even be possible?

To begin, we would acknowledge that the image of the suspicion-addled individual as presented to us by those in media and academia is *not* relevant or generalizable to the mass population. Accurate only within the strictures of the genuinely (more importantly, *conventionally*) ailing individual, the broad mass of cynical, suspicious, Americans cannot be understood in the same way; nor can a mode of cognition or state of consciousness be transposed from the profoundly dysfunctional individual to the mass of politically dysfunctional—that is, estranged—Americans and retain its predictive strength throughout. Neither in his cognitive state nor in his life history is the 28-year-old, high school educated Black man (himself suspicious of the legal system), identical or comparable to the 53-year-old, graduate educated White woman (herself suspicious of the relationship between "the military industrial complex" and "Big Oil") and pretending otherwise does not advance the cause of understanding.

Following this, we would advance beyond our previous attempts at reductionism (e.g., minimizing the phenomenon of suspicion so it may be regurgitated as a simple formula or profile), choosing, instead, to affirm conspiratorialism as an honest attempt by the individual to understand the reality of their experience. We would still need to evaluate each individual instance of conspiratorial ideation to determine whether a person's suspicion hadn't gotten the better of them, but rather than viewing conspiratorial ideation as a pathology—regarding it with mockery, or as cause for worry—for the purposes of understanding we might better consider it as *a process*. Conspiratorialism, or the process of becoming a conspiracy theorist, is not dissimilar (at least in a functional sense, though by no means do I wish to limit the comparison to mere utility) to the transformation undergone by mystics or shamans. Having endured an alteration of his or her own consciousness, the individual acquires some esoteric learning with the expressed intent of returning it to the community for the betterment of all. It should be said that although the method and intensity of alteration is quite different between the two (shamans of the past—and even those in practice today—will subject themselves to great trials of pain, inebriation, or deprivation to achieve the desired effect upon their consciousness), both the conspiracy theorist and the shaman are inexorably transformed by their experience. It might not be wholly inaccurate to admit of a certain, for lack of a better way to state the matter, *psychedelia* inherent to the internet-experience, and so perhaps there remains a further comparison between the shaman and the conspiracy theorist. In fact, for the estranged American, this transformation amounts to a *re-enchantment* of life itself; in the wake of his or her derealization (itself a result of some initial break with *nR*), states of ecstasy and euphoria will soon follow, accompanying the individual's cathartic and ritualistic reanimation of being.

Archaeologist Brian Hayden connects the "*shamanic state of consciousness*" with both ecstatic and mystical experiences (relying on the descriptions of psychiatrists and preeminent students of religious history like Mircea Eliade to do so), and as such, I feel confidently that we can make similar connections between the mind of the shaman and the mind of the conspiracy theorist, ourselves.[46] Such a comparison is not unfounded, though at first blush it strikes us as unwise; attempts to conceptualize today's suspicion-cults in terms of religiousness are quite common, and associating conspiratorial ideation with religiosity would seem to put us on that dangerous, faulty, path. But the shaman is no priest, just as the conspiratorial cults of QAnon, Russian-interference-with-our-democracy, and international White supremacy are not religions. The "second religiousness" hypothesis suggested by Oswald Spengler, thought already to be upon us, may still be (just not in the form many have been quick to suggest). We cannot deny the power of conspiratorial ideation, and of contemporary suspicion-culture, or its ability to drive individuals into radical social—ultimately political—organization. These suspicion-cults

46 Hayden, Brian. 2018. *Shamans, Sorcerers, and Saints*. Smithsonian Institution.

all appear to establish idols and rituals of their own, and in many non-superficial ways give the impression of arising from a pseudo-religious consciousness. But what if the grounds of the phenomenon are not religious *precisely*, but still located, somehow, within a related mode of consciousness? What if we were to ground this relationship not in religiosity, but *in madness itself*? Well, then conspiratorial ideation of the kind evinced by QAnon supporters would be *less* like a cult or religious sect and *more* analogous to a condition of madness—*folie a nombreux*. Not a "second religiousness"—instead, a "*virtual shamanism*", or a "*guardrail psychosis*". If we could achieve this change in perspective, we would understand the conspiratorial man and woman not in terms of pathologies and personal histories, but in terms of his or hers experience of consciousness, a consciousness of madness.

"*Virtual shamanism*", if we can call it such, is entirely facilitated by the technological and economic advancements of the *TIS*, so when we speak of conspiratorial ideation in terms of "*involuntary immersion*" it is intended quite literally. Whereas the shaman is a self-segregating type, the atomizing methodology of life in the West births the individual into a state of isolation that mystics and seers of previous eras were required to self-impose. The originary impetus for exploration may be present or absent, but once initiated, the individual will find themselves traversing what Wouter Kusters calls the "*via mystica psychotica*" (elsewhere in his work he describes it alternatively as "*mad mysticism*").[47] The conspiracy theorist (our virtual shaman) travels the "*via mystica psychotica*" in pursuit of a kind of truth which necessitates a transformation of his or her consciousness. For Kusters, this transformation has four aspects:

1. detachment (p. 173),
2. demagination (p. 195),

47 Kusters, Wouter. 2020. *A Philosophy of Madness*. MIT Press, p. 165.

3. delanguization (p. 213), and
4. dethinking (p. 233).

All of these are effectively ways of deterritorializing the standard conventions of cognitive operation and susceptibilizing oneself, if we can say such a thing, to the negations of mad mysticism. By undergoing detachment, demagination, delanguization, and dethinking, the individual purges himself (or herself) of the typical associations, images, words, and meanings which have come to dominate consciousness so that he (or she) may replace them with "truer things". Consequently, the individual becomes estranged from the inherited social world of duties and roles; so too, will the individual abandon images, icons, and idols, for they can only reify falsehoods; words, phrases, and inherited idioms alike crumble before the *via mystica psychotica*, either becoming expanded and fragmentary (what Kusters terms the "*via metaphorica*", p. 220) or contractive and unifying (due to what Kusters identifies as the "*via multimundiana*", p. 222);[48] all of this culminates in the dissolution of conceptual and perceptual boundaries, or what Kusters calls "*dediscursiving*".

"*Mysticism and madness*" says Kusters, "*with their truth and their experience, are located outside the workings of ordinary life and an ordinary shared language. [They] are concerned*

48 Language is also destabilized (or transformed, for neutrality's sake) through the '*via formica*' (p. 225), wherein meaning is expanded. On this point Kusters says the following: "*We wade around like Don Quixote, not only in terms of meanings but also in terms of language. When all data and meaning vanish into a mad whirlpool of Nothingness, we're still left in the midst of a heap of words, letters, and symbols, without any foundation or background. The words float in the air like fluttering leaves. With no contextual footing, there's no reason not to connect Bonaparte with blown-apart. Nokia becomes associated with "no key". Borders between languages disappear.*"

The naïve, layman's hermeneutics we so often observe in conspiratorial ideation is best understood in terms of this "free spirit of interpretation".

with truth arrived at via insight found in isolation and beyond communality".

And while there is certainly *a kind* of communality available to us through the internet-experience, it is not comparable to that of the lifeworld. Even in his interactions, his exchanges, his inquiries, the conspiracy theorist is his own adjudicator, his own private eye, and in this way, he shares in the experience of mystic madness along with the shaman and the psychotic.

For the conspiracy theorist (as is true once more of the mystic, the shaman, and the psychotic), truth is of the highest value, though it is not "the same kind of truth" sought by others. Kusters has this to say about "truth":

> Mysticism and madness are concerned with an entirely different kind of truth. This truth has to do with an insight or an overwhelming experience that is beyond ordinary reflection and articulation and is of great and inexpressible importance. It is true because it is indisputable. The mystical counterpart to discovery is revelation. The truth of mysticism is not truth about some sub-aspect of the world but rather an expression of the world in its entirety. Instead of a representation of the world, it is fusion with the world. (p. 142).

Shamanism is a dangerous practice—both for the shaman and for his community. Virtual shamanism, then, is no different. This alternative framework I am providing is not intended to aggrandize or exonerate those trafficking in suspicion. That these explorations primarily occur now freely and without consequence in the hyperworld of the internet should give us reason for pause. Not because the pursuit is itself ignoble, but precisely because the very real, very immanent danger is occluded by ease of access and an increasingly apathetic, cavalier, and permissive habit of consumption. Shamanism is definitionally an exclusive role, intended for a select few. Their only real companionship comes in the form of a fear of death or derangement which is never far off. Today's virtual shamans, however, are produced in excess by the cheapening costs and mass availability of advanced communication technologies. It is this innocuousness, though, this unassuming nature of the American man and woman, who, by virtue of merely owning cheaply produced household appliances are thus capable of undertaking a "hero's journey" with no sense of the inherent danger in doing so which ought to concern us more than the kinds of information consumed while in the throes of heroic self-discovery.

When Frodo first agreed to dispose of the One Ring, he at least had some conceptual understanding of the journey he would undertake and the dangers he would thus confront. We should not be concerned by the "threat" posed to our "democracy" by "disinformation"; rather, we should concern ourselves with the consequences of a deteriorating informational ecosystem on the minds and souls of the average American. The conspiracy theorist is neither a terrorist-in-the-making nor a future in-patient at the psych ward. He (or she) may be neurodivergent, while on the other hand, they might be comparatively "normal". Wanderers along the "via mystica psychotica" may be in a state of crisis, but then again so too, have the United States, conservatively, for the last two decades. What the conspiracy theorist is, is an individual caught in an informal process of becoming-mystic, becoming-shaman, and becoming-dissident. This of course presupposes a ritualizing of the internet-experience, a sacralizing of the information it provides, and not simply the aimless wanderings of a bored and disaffected non-agent. Enforcers of the "consens-ist" view of history, on the other hand, may not be so quick to entertain this distinction.

CHAPTER THREE

The Tyranny of Cynical Reason

I follow Peter Sloterdijk in acknowledging the predominance of cynicism as a social mood, and of cynical reason as the reigning cognitive style. Throughout this analysis, we have hinted at and intimated the antecedental role cynical reason plays in the development and nurturing of suspicion-culture; it is only here and now, as we approach the conclusion of our analysis, that we finally arrive upon the point where we might more fully articulate the relationship between cynical reason and suspicion-culture.

Earlier, we took a sociobiological view in understanding American suspicion-culture of the last century and a half. This was necessary for the simple reason that America's political and cultural crises over the past hundred years have resulted in large part due to the deterioration of the ethnic folk stock and its basic presumptions about civic life. Introducing rival people-groups into a polity instigates competition for resources, territories, hierarchies, and discourses. Naturally, we struggle to accept the historical accounts and discursive maneuverings employed by strangers who, being predisposed to a certain habit of life, militate against our own even if it is not their direct intent to do so (though, it must be said, the persuasive force of contemporary social dynamics invariably results in malintent). But this chaotic and violent "artificed state of nature" is not the origin of suspicion-culture. Not in the United States or anywhere else, for that matter. Changes in suspicion-discourse have kept pace with corresponding changes in demography, mutated only by the rapid speed and intensity of recent technological and juridical developments. Our precise moment is highly contingent, far from being a necessary and direct consequence of our foundational axioms. And yet, by following these axioms, we *did* open a field of possibility which included our present moment and so we look to them to excavate (more likely, *approximate*) an original scene of suspicion.

As we identified in the preceding chapter, it is the "self-forgetting" of liberal social theory (culminating at a certain level of civilizational development in the "open society"), and its tendency to "take its own condition of being for granted" which precedes the mad doubt endemic to modern life, engendering, for its part, "suspicion-culture". The problem of suspicion-culture is not simply that the population doubts the intentions of its leadership, or that it doubts the tenets of its religious or social doctrine, or even that individuals doubt themselves (or their neighbors). No. The problem of suspicion-culture is its industrial-scale production of doubt which negates the very possibility of joy. Suspicion-culture is not merely about doubting the intentions or motives of the other, or of disbelieving accounts which purport to explain the unexplainable. Rather, the crisis posed by suspicion-culture is the fact of its schizotizing of the essential domains of human life. The metastasizing powers of reason have allowed it to colonize Man's mindspace, undermining his capacity for uncomplicated enjoyment and easeful participation. In their stead arrives a litany of self-negating justifications. At the juncture between agent and history, reason increasingly permits opportunities for self-abandonment. There are multiple groundings for resisting the propagation of suspicion-culture: liberal hegemony condemns it on pragmatic grounds (e.g., that it foments populism, creates national security risks, "threatens democracy", *et cetera*) but we condemn it on existential grounds (the unfettered promulgation of doubt negates the possibility of a good life).

Reason cloyingly peers into every dark, mad, space like a detective or journalist, rummaging through the private effects of an unknown other(s); because its raison d'être is to "explain" or "account for", reason often (though it must be said, not necessarily) takes the form of an intruder and a body snatcher, playing the role of invasive inquirer into the sacrosanct interior of some unknown object or domain. The reasoning of a *participant*, on the other hand, is of a wholly other phenomenological character; the reason of a neighbor or compatriot carries with it a sense of duty and compassion, and an inviolate desire to deepen or further. The reasoning of a given liberal social theorist is nearly always that of an external account, an extraction or in some slight way, a punitive exploitation. But we need not slip into emotivism or some other such derivation of anti-reason to state our case; reason is neither "bad" nor "wrong", it is merely triumphant. In the wake of its wildly unpredictable over-succeeding, whole domains of human life have been trampled underfoot, left crippled and abandoned in its wake. Negating the primal firstness of life, a move which at first opened plains of economic and geographic domination, has turned what were once coffers of gold into coffins of guilt. Thus, it is the necro-schizoidal reason of the imperial open society (itself an outgrowth of the self-forgetting reason driving hegemonic liberalism's theory of mind) which we ought to organize against, and not simply reason itself. Reason, if properly situated, provides us with the necessary recourse to overthrow its heretical offspring, cynical reason.

(As a brief aside, I would like to say something about the fruit of cynical reason, what is commonly called "nihilism". It is my belief that this so-called nihilism is little more than the revocation of primality—an undermining of the firstness of identity and kinship, but also, an abandonment of the folk account of history. We often speak of nihilism when we wish to interrogate the consequential reign of cynical reason, but to do so, to level the charge of nihilism itself bolsters the universalism of hegemonic liberal social theorizing, giving life to the lie of liberal civilization. Does man reject *all* morality or merely the inherited wisdom of his ancestors? Does *the whole* of life seem worthless to him, or has he simply grown tired of his own life, and of those spheres most familiar to him? Insofar as the open society is, itself, a stand-in for the universalism of theory, then yes, when we reject liberal social theorizing, we are also rejecting "all life itself" for there often appears to be no life outside of the open society. Of course, *there can only be* life outside of the open society, a conclusion which we have drawn from our own investigation into the matter. The open society, liberal democracy, whatever we call it, is the proverbial last stop for organic living; everything about our post-war lifestyle is synthetic—from its base presumptions, its manner of reproduction, its aspirations—how could it not but spell our doom?)

Reason militates against superstition, just as the latter does the former. Perhaps it always has been as such, after all, the dichotomy between *religio* and *superstitio* (an analogue of the very same discourse we are presently engaged in) is nearly as old as the Western tradition itself. Considering this fact, we might ease our polemic against liberalism somewhat, as the problem of authorship (manifesting as it so often does in the dichotomies of rationality/irrationality, reason/prejudice, and religio/superstitio) clearly precedes it. What we observe in the Enlightenment version of this tradition is merely a recapitulation of the same problem only this time, on scientific groundings. Contemporary psychology (which is to say, theories developed following the Second World War) has certainly championed this dichotomy between science (rationality/reason) and religion (irrationality/superstition) when attempting a definition of "superstition"; though his paradigm is now regarded as little more than a relic of mid-century psychological theorizing, B.F. Skinner's work on the concept of superstition succinctly captures the 20th century iteration of this Enlightenment tradition. Skinner famously wrote about the "superstitious" behavior observed in his cherished test subject, the pigeon.

Of his findings, Skinner wrote the following:

> The experiment might be said to demonstrate a sort of superstition. The bird behaves as if there were a causal relation between its behavior and the presentation of food, although such a relation is lacking. There are many analogies in human behavior. Rituals for changing one's fortune at cards are good examples. A few accidental connections between a ritual and favorable consequences suffice to set up and maintain the behavior in spite of many unreinforced instances. The bowler who has released a ball down the alley but continues to behave as if she were controlling it by twisting and turning her arm and shoulder is another case in point. These behaviors have, of course, no real effect upon one's luck or upon a ball half way down an alley, just as in the present case the food would appear as often if the pigeon did nothing—or, more strictly speaking, did something else.[1]

While later research would severely cripple the authority of Skinner's interpretation, the true legacy of this study was not in its scientific accuracy or empirical rigor, but in how perfectly it encapsulates the imperial liberal's narcissism of necessity. While Skinner thought he was demonstrating something profound about avian psychology, something which he would by inference seek to attribute to human psychology, what he recorded was in fact the over-eagerness of reason to suffocate

1 B. F. Skinner, "Superstition in the Pigeon," *Journal of Experimental Psychology* #38, 1947.

knowledge (and, if left untrammeled, even life itself) through arrogance and the nervous will to explain. This is the paranoia of reason (manifesting in its final formulation as schizotizing suspicion-culture), which with each passing generation of Enlightenment conformity, seeks fresh "survivors" (e.g., superstitions, rival traditions, modes of being and of knowledge derived primally and thus in harmony with the firstness of pre-existing folkways) to extirpate, aided by the massively expanding machine of compliance: the managerial technocratic society.

(Allowing for another digression, the behavioral psychology of B.F. Skinner presents as an ethno-metanarrative of its own, if not, at the least, the expression of a particularly technocratic desire: the desire to bury man's agency, eliminate his critical faculties, and to render him subordinate to the ascendant post-war institutions of authority. At a time when continental psychology—via psychoanalysis—was uncovering the cavernous idiosyncrasies of consciousness, in rushed Anglo-Saxon psychology to quickly reassert the supremacy of superficiality. A psychological framework such as Skinner's proved rather adept at offering a scientific means by which the emerging technocratic order might implement its preferred methodologies of social engineering. Politically this proved quite useful, especially when it comes to delicately navigating the dual implementation of conflicting social values, such as patriotism and demographic replacement—any man can be an American, presuming he was never any kind of man at all in the first place. What Popper sought to accomplish politically via piecemeal engineering, Skinner sought through technocratically implemented models of operant conditioning—both of which were not only compatible with but forerunners to the contemporary Sunstein-ian methodology of "nudging".)

As a concept, "superstition" has taken on a meaning quite particular and out of step with its original usage, though in some ways, the heart of the idea has managed to sustain its pulse.

Presently, we use the word "superstition" when we wish to invoke the stupid, the parochial, or the anachronistic; that which we deem "superstition" is in fact pre-personal, the product of an anthropomorphic tendency (we see objects and events as we see ourselves) which conspires with autobiographical narrativization (we account for objects and events in terms of our own experience), thus establishing it as the starkest and, from the point of view of political control, most troubling example of social opacity available to us within hypermodern liberalism. It is this inavailability of experience which antagonizes liberal social theoreticians, offering itself as a fatal paradox—a paradox in that the individual is both the fulfilment and negation of liberal social theory. The rational individual may freely subject himself to the machinations of the open society or he may choose to reject it on rationally self-justifying grounds. Or he may utilize his rationality to collapse into irrationalism, thereby undermining the liberal project entirely. Is it even *absolutely* obvious to us when an individual is engaged in one strategy or the other? But of course, by asking the question we are reifying the very dichotomy which, in truth, requires detonation, not explication. That which the open society can achieve at industrial scale through the leveraging of networks of institutional power, all but crippling the masses of men, Man himself may still overcome. Through choice and free thought, those native faculties exalted by liberalism (only to be dismissed, in a confused and muddled way by neoliberalism), Man defeats the joylessness of suspicion-culture. Choice and thought, rational faculties, informed first and foremost by the so-called "irrational" and "superstitious".

The irrational, even schizophrenic, black box of individual experience—particularly (though by no means *exclusively*) that of the *exceptional* individual—alone resists the totalitarian influence of the open society's institutional power. Superstition is therefore subjected to the principle of enmity, and as such, it is almost exclusively used to describe practices or beliefs held by "bad" people (those we seek to disenfranchise). The meaning of "superstition" appears then to be determined according to belongingness, and therefore has its most direct utility in othering (as true now, perhaps, as it was during the time of Cicero who famously sought to abolish superstition).[2]

Having just invoked Cicero, let us continue in this direction a little further. In the ancient world, the debate between *religio* and *superstitio* was a debate over what constituted proper conduct and attitude regarding civic and religious practices. Paranoia, fearfulness, obsequiousness/slavishness, falsity, supernaturalism—these were (and to many today, *still are*) the marks of superstition, while *religio* was virtually synonymous with "proper adherence to/reverence for" the dominant or normative religion. Charges of impropriety were leveled against all—by the Romans against the Christians, by the Romans against other Roman subjects, by the Christians against pagans/Romans, and so on. This practice continues well into our own time. Despite its long history, a core concept of what technically constitutes "superstition" is still unavailable to us, precisely because its use was heavily contingent on conflict or confrontation between people-groups with differing accounts of the religious experience. Today, the two (religion and superstition) are no longer considered distinct; rather they are regarded as effectively one and the same, with the juxtaposition no longer occurring between properly or improperly held religious beliefs and practices, but between reason (rationalism) and prejudice (irrationalism).[3] Both expressions of this discourse, however, share in a central tension:

2 Cicero, *De Natura Deorum* II, 28 (32), quoted in Wagenvoort, Hendrik (1980). *Pietas: selected studies in Roman religion.* Leiden, NetherlandsL Brill. P. 236.

3 We might say that while this new juxtaposition does not occur along conventionally religious lines, it is still concerned with conduct and norms, specifically the conduct and norms immanent to our rival conceptions of secular, rationalist humanism.

the challenge posed by attempting an adherence to older folk ways in the face of emerging civilizational developments. The early distinction between *religio* and *superstitio* clearly foretells the later Enlightenment era recapitulation of the debate, a debate which we are still engaged in only this time, under hypermodern conditions of unceasing abstraction, calamity, and intensity.

For Popper, as we have noted already, the great historical debate has always been between that of the open society and the closed society. We find ourselves however in uncomfortable (but not complete) agreement with Deleuze and Guattari—that in fact, the great historical rivalry is between the paranoid (*religio*, reason, rationality) and the schizophrenic (*superstitio*, prejudice, irrationality).[4] After all, the beating heart of the open society *is* its paranoia—with its commitment to ethics, its paranoid fear of unjust expulsion or exclusion by a hostile and "irrational" other—while the self-constituting exclusivity of the closed society, with its intense focus on ontology and metaphysics clearly derives its generative power from a more schizophrenic mode of self-construction. Reason, particularly in the form known as *cynical* reason, is the great maestro of paranoid cognition due to the very fact of its restlessness; cynical reason agitates *because it is, itself, agitated*. We will say more on this, but for the moment let us set it aside.

Consider the following archetypal antinomies: the priest and the shaman; the philosopher and the artist; the politician and the folk hero; a given social field cannot shut one or the other out without risking its own untimely demise, and yet the two energies constantly struggle to assert themselves or at the

4 I invoke psychiatric language though I intend their meanings to be *libidinal* and not *pathological*. The paranoid libido of rationality is merely the characteristically productive energy immanent to that movement, just as schizophrenia is the libido of irrationality. At their extremes, each mode of production will inhabit its stereotypically dysfunctional form but unless clearly stated, the use of both terms should be understood as occurring in a normative context.

least, escape the machinations of the other. Further examples of this contest abound: the strait-laced corporate-type chafes at the "loose" and "undisciplined" habits of the creative. Law enforcement officers loathe (and are loathed by) the hippy, the vagrant, and the reformer. The constituting powers of the paranoiac give form and definition to an entity while the dissolving powers of the schizophrenic threaten to erode the very boundaries of identity. That erosion, however, is a necessary step on the path toward reconstitution (a fact which remains underappreciated by both sides). While the paranoiac is primarily motivated by the will to life, the willingness to give oneself over to the salvific power of reconstitution is often—and particularly in the most crucial and definitive moments of one's life—the path by which the will to life fully realizes itself. The paranoiac's ego defenses are triggered by this fact, as the safeguarding of the ego can only be achieved by its temporary dissolution (or suspension). The schizophrenic (again, invoked libidinally and not pathologically) holds a privileged position in society owing to its catalyzing power, but it is because of this immanent and unpredictable combustibility that schizophrenic energies must be constrained (or ordered). This imposition provokes the schizophrenic's defenses as well, as the external introduction of form (e.g., the law, hygiene, scarcity, and so on) is perceived as a threat to the very will to life. Contra Popper once more, the resolution to this rivalry is not found in abandoning Platonic social theory, rather, it is through embracing Plato's thought that we might resolve this tension. Specifically, through embracing Plato's notion of justice: a place for every kind, according to its kind.

Superstition represents that which has survived, that which persists. Now, not everything that survives is something we would wish to see persevere, this much is true. But from the point of view of a skeptical outsider (the paranoiac), it may not be possible to distinguish the useful and desirable from the harmful and disgusting. For reason to enter a space of superstition without disturbing its interior law, it must do so as a student enters a renowned master's dojo: with a deep and abiding reverence. Reason that can sublimate itself to the interior law of superstition can deepen that tradition without destroying it, correct/improve its faulty assumptions without replacing it altogether. Often it is the case that "success" is not something reducible to a concrete and constantly reproducible mechanism; we can provide strategies and methodologies, yes, but these can only create the pre-conditions or the bare necessities of success, not the success-object itself (e.g., the desired result). It is up to the agent himself to secure the success-object. But he cannot do so without proper guidance and preparation. This is one such example which justifies calls to curtail the enthusiastic reason of the paranoiac: for the overcoding of pre-existing folk-accounts risks erasing irretrievable wisdom.

A libido of paranoiac-rationality seeks the overcoding of all interiors, the result of which we may call the *"madness of reason"*. Reason has a psychosis of its own, one that is true to its own logic and character; it is not the psychosis of the schizophrenic, for the *"reason of madness"* is more a mechanism or principle of dissolution rather than a strategy or grounds for organization (thereby solidifying it as non-arborescent in constitution). The madness of reason (as an overheated imperialism of logic) seeks to bend other traditions towards itself, mutating them until achieving a final Borg-like state of compliance. It coerces this conformity by forcing rival traditions to abandon their own prejudices (said differently, *axioms*) in favor of those prejudices most amenable to its needs. Neoliberal democracy makes excellent political use of the paranoiac-libido, but it also harnesses the schizophrenic-libido to this end as well. Contemporary liberal democracy marshals its own schizophrenic-libido as a kind of anti-power, a generative power in service of death, eroding the vitality and coherence of the other to achieve this subjugation. Coercion and erosion; deconstruction and dissolution; formidable in its dexterity, the open society wields both "essences" (paranoia and schizophrenia) in defense of itself.

And just what are liberal democracy's prejudices? What form(s) does this anti-power of schizo-libidinal-irrationality ultimately take? Liberalism's fixation on the individual engenders it with a totalitarianism all its own, distinct, and somewhat more difficult to identify (particularly from the perspective of a participant within liberal democracy) than those political models most associated with tyranny (e.g., fascism, communism, national socialism). The first such prejudice would be liberal democracy's preoccupation with liberty: the individual's right to liberty over time becomes a command to liberate oneself, before ending as a condemnation. Exalting individual liberty initially occurred as a development of a new kind of life, and therefore also as a polemic against the old monarchical regime, but once liberal social theorizing ascended to the level of hegemon it could only militate against *the fact of life itself*, and not merely the fact of *some other style of living*. The prominence of abortion (and increasingly of euthanasia, too) speaks to this fact: we no longer seek to throw off the yoke of the king and the church (or overthrow some other social constraint, for that matter), but to liberate ourselves from the very conditions of our existence.

One's right to be skeptical of superstition, to be doubtful, and to *constitute himself (or herself) on the very basis of this doubt* becomes—under liberal democracy—an obligation, a duty, to do so, or worse, a presumption. This is a second prejudicial axiom of liberal democracy. The sense in which human civilization rides along a wave of perpetual progress, continual growth and development, *et cetera*, is a misguided one, for what we are in fact perceiving is the degree to which *human life itself* has become subordinated to the liberal principle of *"the project"*. Life is no longer for itself; rather it is for the continuance of some liberal axiom. Take, for example, the circumstance of motherhood: a woman carefully plans her first pregnancy, hoping that she has a son. She does this, not out of a reverence for or appreciation of the masculine person, but to raise him as the first feminist man of her line. In doing so, the expectant mother makes a shrine to the madness of reason out of her yet-unborn child's life. As a result of this very same desire, her own life assumes a providence otherwise reserved for the traditional institutions of pastoral power. Means become ends. The individual, long before arriving to a consciousness of the circumstances which formed him (or her), is subjected to this ontological suspicion, making of his or her life an operation—a campaign—against one's own native identity and thus, as well, against one's folk ways of being. This is only the first of many estrangements wrought upon Man by liberalism and the open society.

> "We had a daughter not to honor God, or to share in the experience of the beauty of life, but so that she could go into STEM and inspire other girls to go into STEM, too."

Hence the joylessness of life. Human life as the reification of some liberal prejudice is part of the self-negation we have discussed from the very beginning of this work; it is not merely the censorious self-persecuting psychic-insert of alien occupation which tyrannizes man's mind. No: It is the fact of his (or her) life being sacrificed—before birth—to satisfy the prejudices of liberal democracy which themselves wreak the greatest havoc on human consciousness.

Having firmly rooted ourselves in this polemical posture, we may, briefly, attempt to applaud this form of liberal democracy. (We have been quite thoroughgoing in our critique, after all.) If there were a virtue to be found within the open society, we might locate it within its forward-thinkingness (as opposed to the closed society's stifling preoccupation with history). Posturing itself in this way allows the open society to deftly outmaneuver its political opponents. This fact is often discussed under the euphemistic discourse of "progress". When we speak of "progress" (as in technological progress, cultural progress, or as an act performed by history), we are not speaking of an ontic reality or a metaphysical necessity (though that is often what we perceive it to be). We are in fact speaking of an ego-buffering aggregation of tendencies: the will to self-disassemble, a predisposition toward novelty (and thus, naivety), a constitutional disagreeableness and consequently, an expectation (and even lusting after) of conflict. "Progress" is a type, or a form, or expression—a *style* if you will. And it necessarily militates against others. But even liberal democracy's strengths bring us back, ultimately, to that which we condemn: this forward orientation comes at the expense of the constituent elements of identity. This is why, for instance, a White English child can be stabbed to death in his own neighborhood by a foreign national and his parents will beg others not to "politicize" his death by calling into question the political factors which led to the child's untimely end. The well-being of the folk population is the sacrifice made to keep the open society from collapsing in on itself. Under the tyranny of the open society, one is free to doubt any tradition he wishes, so long as it is not the tradition of liberal democracy. (The most important prejudice/axiom of the open society, after all, is intolerance qua Marcuse and Popper.) True joy is not possible wherever the pursuit of a genuine knowledge of self and divinity is denied. Quite ironic then, how the patron saint of the open society, Socrates, who is possibly best known for his love of self-knowledge, is so often invoked (whether by Karl Popper or other advocates of unfettered liberal democracy) despite the open society's sustained attack on the firstness of identity (the necessary precursor to self-knowledge). We might say, then, that "progress" is cynicism expressed *viz* political action.

Cynicism as a prevailing sentiment arose from the liberal "projectivizing" of life: this much is true, and yet there is still more to the story. While the liberal Enlightenment tradition of doubt/skepticism is a constant threat to the stability of rival traditions, it is merely one of the cascading waves which contribute to the reign of cynical reason. Liberalism's abject failure to realize the promise of sustained prosperity and unobstructed individual fulfillment is not only widely recognized, but the reverberating depths of this failure are ever intensifying. We no longer believe, truly, in liberal precepts (hence our cynicism) and yet we are dependent on them all the same (or at least, we depend on the institutions tasked with safeguarding those precepts) in order to sustain our own existence (hence, as well, our guilt). Liberal social theory proved itself other than a panacea, for it was not the engine behind Western wealth and success. The true cause of liberal hegemony was its folk stock, not its philosophy alone (as if theory could arise from out of nowhere). But, owing to the self-forgetting of liberal theory, we have thrown the proverbial baby out with the bathwater. We have failed, but not only that, we have consciousness of this failure and yet we are unable (or unwilling) to step over this failure. The open society has failed, but then again, so has everything else. Why is there nothing but misery if we are history's winners? Why do we suffer disbelief if we have finally secured the answers to life's mysteries? Why, if our homes are so filled with consumer goods, and our refrigerators are stocked full of food, why then do we feel so hollow? In truth, liberal democracy is no longer even capable of providing life's material necessities; the presumption that membership in the open society would result in full bellies and fuller wallets is no longer plausible. The collapse of liberalism's remaining state rival (Soviet Russia) exposed the oligarchical nature of the open society, with the intervening decades only reinforcing that fact. Enlightenment liberalism's demystifying power left its ethnic stock fatigued and hollow, overcoding their particularist experience of life, thereby transforming them into perfect (or perfectly lifeless) "universalized" subjects.

The 20th century was nearly a fatal one for liberal democracies around the world, with the great wars (and their consequences) coming close to swallowing the European continent whole. Were it not for the vitally lifesaving transfusion of Central and Eastern European migrant intellectuals, the long-standing Enlightenment tradition of cynicism might have died on the vine. An effect of this transfusion, however, was a psychological mutation which transformed the European/American cosmopolitanism of simple liberal democracy into the global village of the open society (transforming, along with it, the "style" of Western cynicism). The cynicism of "classical" Enlightened liberal social theory was of the order of a simulation, constructing a facsimile identity to augment (and later, supersede) the native identities already present. For a time, the "unmasking" cynicism of early Enlightenment thinking produced tremendous philosophical, juridical, and artistic works—a great deal of which are as synonymous with "the West" as any of its prior achievements—and may have represented the peak of an authentically "Western" tradition. Cynicism of the post-war neoliberal stage through to the present day, on the other hand, is of the order of a dissimulation, for today's liberal democracies are populated by those who claim to have dispensed with their originary prejudices and folk histories, but who in fact leverage them for material and political gain at the expense of the folk stock native to these spaces. Previous iterations of European cynicism had a wide range of targets which they could subject to the revelatory power of (cynical) reason: religion, politics, art, the sciences, literature, and so on. The cynicism of post-war neoliberal social theorizing, though, has a far narrower scope of interest: the Western ethnos itself. Whereas the cynicism of classical liberal thought was the cynicism of an invested participant, one who sought to enrich and advance his tradition, neoliberal cynicism is motivated by envy, resentment, and vulgar self-preservation (the parasite as opposed to the participant). Hypermodern suspicion-culture has seen the elevation of "bad faith" to the position of discursive king. Discourse is now unending, though genuine communication and understanding are seemingly in permanent short supply. Reason—once seen as the royal road to truth—has become but one more worn-down path to power (real or imagined). Perhaps it was ever as such.

That Western-style liberal democracy was no longer the exclusive home of a family of ethno-metanarratives but rather became a nesting ground for the most paranoiac of alien ethno-metanarratives led it more fully into the cynical mode of self-preservation (as the ferocious contest of life had now taken a dramatic turn for the worse). Liberalism already rested upon an ontology of violence but following the inclusion of radically particularistic and intolerant people-groups, themselves escaping persecution (others simply escaping the harsh conditions of their own circumstance), funneled into Anglophone society the intensification of flows and desires, culminating in an even more corrosive type of cynical reason. Looking back from our hypermodern vantage point, it seems now that the legacy of cynical reason was that of the war of all against all and of self-abandonment, culminating paradoxically, in a fever of self-annihilating conformity. It is also the tradition of psychological imprisonment. But as we have already declared throughout the course of our analysis, this scene is only the latest in a chain of developments spawning from the original cynical permutation wrought by the early phases of secularization (culminating in the Enlightenment era). Let us focus one last time on the meaning of this original cynicism, and its influence on the development of suspicion-culture.

As Sloterdijk says of cynicism, it…

> …is enlightened false consciousness. It is that modernized, unhappy consciousness, on which enlightenment has labored both successfully and in vain. It has learned its lessons in enlightenment, but it has not, and probably was not able to, put them into practice. Well-

> off and miserable at the same time, this consciousness no longer feels affected by any critique of ideology; its falseness is already reflexively buffered.[5][6]

No one may harm us but ourselves. We are immune and yet we are barren. The triumph of cynical reason is also the death of joy; it is the ascent of the schizoid over the common man, or rather the subsumption of the common man into a social pathology of schizoid-like conduct. The schizoid is the prototypical atomized individual, a consciousness of pure isolated ideation whose only reference point is within himself. Fairbairn described the schizoid as being characterized by an air of omnipotence and grandiosity, and so when we consider this personality style in full view of what we are calling suspicion-culture (and in fact this observation is even more true of conspiratorial ideation, specifically) the characterization strikes as even more relevant. Who else would dare investigate "the New World Order" or challenge "the Matrix" but the God-like shut-in? If one presumes a reality dictated by violent covert action, one in which inquisitive busybodies

5 Sloterdijk, Peter. *Critique of Cynical Reason*, translation by Michael Eldred; foreword by Andreas Huyssen (Minneapolis: University of Minnesota Press, 1987), pp. 5–6. (Theory and History of Literature; v. 40) Original: *Kritik der zynischen Vernunft*, 1983.

6 Sloterdijk's definition of cynicism/cynical reason could double as a description of the folk-historian (conspiracy theorist) *and* the consensist-historian (conspiracy denier), thereby drawing our identification of the one (cynicism) with the other (suspicion-culture) ever more tightly together. Ten minutes spent watching the United States press secretary (anyone, though for maximum effect I recommend a recent one) field questions from the press is all the confirmation one need if he/she hopes to see how Sloterdijk's description of cynicism applies to those individuals and institutions tasked with the ignoble responsibility of regime apologia. They are on the side of power, self-consciously so, and perform their role admirably. The same self-satisfaction can be observed among the less scrupulous (or merely less cognitively adroit) conspiracy theorists who, being neurotically allergic to the regime's account of *any* event are similarly locked into a trench warfare of skepticism.

who get "in too deep" suddenly find themselves on the wrong side of a prison cell (or worse), and soldiers on in the face of what they have surely understood to be—even if only in an intellectual way—*certain doom*, then one simply *must* be governed by a cavalier ego. Furthermore, the non-relationality of the schizoid person influences their conspiratorialism, for the scope of their investigations are always far narrower, and far less interconnected (the opaque parental-image formed in childhood often results in a diminished capacity to "know" the minds of others. Thus, the schizoid's social maps rarely capture the motivations and intentions of others. Such an impairment renders conspiratorial ideation powerless and incoherent). The congenitally schizoid man or woman does not know joy because they do are too idiosyncratic, too "self-sufficient", too apathetic, but also too *satisfied* by their own internal experiences. Schizoid man does not know the joys of social living, nor does he ever experience its boundary-dissolving rituals—rituals which build anew from that which it had just destroyed (e.g., marriage, parenthood, and so on). Man, as he lives today, enmeshed against his will within the technocratic open society, suffers a similar condition: he is "schizo-tized" by the incessant impingements of liberal social theory, "psychoticized" by the cruelty of his rapidly degrading and decadent environment, and the fundamentals of his life are decided, increasingly, by impersonal and often unaccountable bureaucrats, thereby analogizing the facts of his social experience to the interior of a conspiracy theory. Hypermodern cynicism is, in its social consequences, indistinguishable from a cluster A personality disorder[7] (hence the extreme dysfunction of contemporary

7 Enlightenment cynicism unmasked its opponent to "educate" and "civilize" him, to bring into light that which had languished in superstition. Contra its progenitor, hypermodern cynicism unmasks its opponent, unveils, and "demystifies" (in the language of this still mutating strand, *decolonizes*) it to humiliate and destroy it. Hypermodern cynicism is simply a will to power dressed up in exhausted formalities.

suspicion-culture/conspiratorial ideation).[8]

As for cynicism in its older expressions, I ask you the following: what were the "wars of religion" if not a prototypical form of suspicion-culture? Or the separation of church and state? Or the colonization and subsequent individuating of North America? Or the Suffragette movement? Was not the whole of American history prior to the 20th century (and European history in the handful of centuries preceding that), in fact, not an ode to suspicion-culture? Which is to say, were not all these events driven by the desire to discover—or usurp—sovereignty? That the Western tradition of skepticism has taken a rather abrupt (and suicidal) turn as of late does not negate the longer history of outwardly facing liberal skepticism. Undoubtedly 18th century Man felt differently about himself and his skeptical endeavoring's than 21st century Man does today—if only because the inquiry was then conducted on *his* terms, for now, man finds himself the subject of *another's* inquiry. Nevertheless, both men find themselves partaking in the same Enlightenment project: doubt.

The Parallax View of Truth

Does human suffering, or rather, the discourse around and our conceptualization of human suffering, precipitate our material circumstances or is it merely a consequence of them? In the present hypermodern period, our material circumstances are formulated by overproduction, resulting from an attitude of production for its own sake (the ethic of perpetual motion). Wherever one looks he sees abundance: too many consumer goods, too many television programs, too much food (which then leads to too much trash, and subsequently, too much guilt). Too many opportunities then lead to too many *missed*

8 "Cluster A" personality disorders, as detailed in the "*Diagnostic and Statistical Manual of Mental Disorders*", include paranoid personality disorder, schizoid personality disorder, and schizotypal personality disorder.

opportunities, which, over a long enough period, results in a conceptual obliteration of the very idea of "opportunity" *itself*. And should the social field (inclusive of the individual's perceptual field) be comprised of too many images of sexuality, themselves made too freely accessible? What follows is the near collapse of sexual conduct—particularly that conduct which is of the eusocial and replenishing variety. Scarcity, as a material instantiation of the principle of constraint, *fortifies*, while abundance *obliterates* (abundance, which is generative of *ease*, is the great liquidator of constraint-based ethics). Both produce a suffering of their own, but while one may lift themselves up (or be uplifted from) conditions of scarcity or poverty, there is neither a greater view nor greener pasture to ascend towards once one has entrenched him or herself within a space of abundance. The only remaining spaces of domination and exploration which still exist within a post-scarcity paradigm are those of the *internal* or *psychic* spaces, which abundance reflexively buffers against. (Abundance is ego-inflating, thereby cheapening the currency of consciousness—thought.)

At the level of large territories like the nation-state and the empire, one cannot so easily declare the complete geographical predominance of overproduction-pain (abundance) or underproduction-pain (scarcity), for the nature of some locales are unlike those of other regions (e.g., rural/urban life, tropical/arctic ecologies, and so on), leading to differing expressions of the crisis of materialism. As a fact of technological society, however, abundance is the socio-perceptual law of hypermodernity, consequently overriding the on-the-ground facts of individual communities and their discrete experiences. Spaces of scarcity and constraint (and the folkways which accompany them) are therefore seen as oppressive, something to escape from (causing the population to flee into the arms of the open society). The success of the neoliberal open society, then, is not in its lofty abstract conceptualization of Man, nor in its purportedly superior social theory or mode of political organization, rather it is in the way it seduces Man—appealing to those base, primitive, aspects of human consciousness, triggering a borderline psychotic lustfulness.

It isn't that we have permanently abolished scarcity—in fact, we may soon arrive upon a time of long overdue refamiliarization—rather, it is that we no longer possess a strong, ritualized, concept of lack or absence (which are distinct from scarcity; when it comes to desire, somewhere, elsewhere, there is always *more*). Owing to this, we have only grown more hysterical towards notions of deprivation. Subjectively, it is experienced as tyrannical (even if it is only temporary). We have inherited an alienated notion: a discourse which originated in privation, and now reflects itself in our characterization of suffering. Everything is meaningless, there is no reason to live, nothing is true, so on and so forth. Pure histrionics.

It is true that we are undergoing a crisis of meaning, and that truth is in fact imperiled. People struggle to find certainty or a purpose that would keep them upright and stiff-lipped in the face of life's cruelty. But none of this happens because we lack meaning *in our own* lives, or because we find *life itself* to be inherently meaningless, or even because we no longer accept the primacy of truth. There are, in fact, *too many* truths, *too much* meaning, and *too many* reasons for pursuing the telos or style of life of another'. The problem of so-called impoverishment (in truth, *impairment*) is secondary to the eclipsing of the particular by neoliberal democracy and its open society (the forces responsible for and thus productive of this "impoverishment"). The suffering of American (or Western) men, women, and children is the suffering-experience of the discarded locales and particularities in the face of the imperial and universal—it is the suffering induced by the unassimilable big Other. What we *truly* lack, *specifically*, are reasons (and the social infrastructure necessary to reinforce them) to carry on our own traditions, and so we all, collectively and yet also as isolated strangers, collapse into the Lacanian Symbolic and its reserve of ego-production, subjectivated as it were by the open society (remade, or better yet, *mutated* by the meddlesome and anti-human social engineering of the present neoliberal democratic order).

While we are accustomed to and prejudicially *presume* abundance (alternatively, "*availability*") as an axiom, we still do not yet appreciate its consequences. Abundance attracts rival people-groups who do not participate in the long-standing conceptual and ethical folk tradition, a fact which is axiomatically negated, or occluded, by liberal prejudice. Liberalism's core delusion, its will to self-forget (more accurately, self-deceive), is a seductive one: not only does liberalism compel its folk constituency to delude themselves, but it also entangles the other in the very same movement of delusion. The alien himself is complicit, a force for reinforcing folk self-forgetting—an integral component to the ritual of self-annihilation. In the face of competing ethno-metanarratives, wherein the alien elements are privileged not only by the organic prejudice of novelty but also the ideological prejudice of the open society (which privileges the alien as a form of pro-active self-defense against folk axioms/prejudices), the reason of folk tradition collapses at the feet of pluri-racial neoliberalism. The "why" which sustains, for example, Italian-American Roman Catholicism or Ulster-Scot Protestantism, struggles to assert itself in the face of neoliberalism's orgiastic panorama of destruction and pleasure. Folk traditions of virtually all kinds inevitably suffer the same fate: overcoded at the hands of technocratic democracy in an act which replaces (through impairment) the telos of folk-identity with that which is compatible with the desires of the present technocratic order. The abundance of discourses and cultures, arising from an abundance of people-groups, necessarily reduces to tribal conflict, as the intersection between sociobiology and politics creates a fruitful biopolitical resource for the regime. Truth and meaning, as well as purpose and dignity, are therefore made casualties of the open society and its cynical, antisocial ethic of self-preservation. Because the ethos of the open society is enmity and militancy against folk organization, it distorts these virtues, instrumentalizing them, bending them to its will. The image of the open society as a global village, as being everywhere all at once, the impression or presumption of its essentiality or primary-ness, lends itself to the prejudice of abundance, reinforcing and fortifying it once more in the minds of the governed. To partake of truth, meaning, purpose, and dignity *authentically* and *eusocially* necessitates self-extrication from the ontology of the open society.

Rootedness, we might also say belongingness, is the ontological pre-requisite for truth-seeking. For all of liberalism's claims toward the objective, e.g., the scientific method and so on, it has lost the right to make such claims about itself, most perceptibly since the Second World War but almost certainly prior to that event. The early mode(s) of Enlightenment/liberal theorizing succeeded because the ethnic stock responsible for birthing them had not yet slipped into the mode of self-forgetting. But once they did, its fatal conceit began unraveling. Liberalism's tendency to self-negate, to doubt (productive of its view from nowhere) in fact inhibits truth-seeking because one must first possess an orientation before he can take direction. When man first took note of the position of the stars he did so with a knowledge and awareness of the plot of ground beneath his feet; the stars and constellations themselves, the planets and their movements, these were all unknowable without a primary knowledge—a knowledge of self and circumstance. The great heroes of terrestrial globalization, those illustrious seafaring European men who discovered the New World, accomplished this feat precisely because of their commitment to the first things of life (faith and folk).

The universal is only intelligible, articulable, knowable, through participation and enmeshment with some particular; the first things of human experience ground man, orient him, situating him in a time and place constituted by meaning and history; he begins from some real and authentic place, allowing him to extend outward (both his social space, but also his own body and consciousness). Social particularity and the community it offers up to us are but the first building blocks on the way towards this grander conceptual understanding. The spirit of particularity, once wedded to the intellect of the universal, together form the engine which carries man far beyond his parochial borders.

Access to what I am calling here "*the parallax view of truth*"—which I believe to be the antidote to hypermodern cynicism (perhaps known better by its other name, "the post-truth society")—is only possible if one is operating first from an authentic and ritual-bound perspective, one capable of situating itself among nests of perspectives without nervously castigating (or over-congratulating) itself. Pluralism has long been a fact of social reality; it merely took us some centuries for this to manifest as the crippling nervous syndrome of consciousness we now experience it to be. But even this uneasiness or squeamishness around the notion of truth, as understandable an experience as one can conceive, was itself massaged into existence. It need not be the case that European or American society, for instance, ought to necessarily grow queasy or lose its nerve in the face of some other people-group's tradition or claim to truth. Only by finally arriving at this outlandish expectation for European and American folkishness to abolish itself do we discover the *"non-non-telos"*, as it were, of the open society: neoliberalism's self-forgetting is more like a form of self-erasure, obliterating folkish firstness, thereby destroying the only reliable path to universal knowledge (and truth). Because the open society is a simulacrum of social order, it cannot offer a real path to truth, much less truth itself—only artificed paralogical cliches which anesthetize thought. Under neoliberal democracy there is but one articulable truth, and that is of the ultimate goodness—and necessity—of the open society (that paranoiac cult of the particular; masquerading as a universal intellect, it finds itself locked in a life-or-death struggle against the remaining, in its view *rivaling*, social orders).

What I speak of here (the rivalry between a unified folk particularity-universality and the para-universality of the open society) is the difference between a hyperopic morality and a myopic one, or in other words, a view of the Good which is far-sighted as opposed to the near-sightedness of (neo) liberal democracy. Now, as we have already noted, the open society (by its own admission) is Good-less; it is the posture of self-defense made into a political theory, one more explicitly Schmittian than earlier modes of liberal social organizing (owing to its emergence out of liberalism's rivalry with fascism and communism). The open society represents a "matured" liberalism, one that has seen the scales fall from its eyes, thus eschewing grand vision-making for incrementalism and crowd control. Now as a theory we might go ahead and accept the supposed Good-lessness of the open society, but as a political practice we must acknowledge that it is a model executed by people who are, themselves, motivated by some view of the Good (hence the dichotomy I have presented between moral hyperopia and moral myopia).

In effect, neoliberalism's "Good" is the "Good" of the paranoid neurotic, and as such ought properly to be understood as tyrannical (representative itself of a well-known type: the myopic authority who says, *"this is for your own good (even though we both know damn well enough that it isn't)"*. Put differently, it is the authority proper to the short-sighted egotist; problems are pre-formulated while solutions are rarely if ever re-evaluated (merely re-applied at ever escalating levels of intensity and caustic irrationality). We might liken it to a kind of *political determinism*, for its social parameters appear to function according to a model of (deranged) predestiny: folk consciousness is necessarily genocidal (thereby entitling others to pre-emptively attack it); suspicion of oligarchic power is always irrational, paranoid, and therefore unjustified (thus validating the diminution of the civilian population's axiomatic legal protections); the Good cannot be discovered (therefore we must divert the whole of political economy toward disenfranchising and impoverishing potential threats); freedom is the highest moral good (and can only be secured by erasing the everyday firstness of human life); these—there may well be more examples—are the constituent elements of the open society's political determinism, predicated on the defect of reasoning I am calling myopic morality. It is not that the perspectivism of particularity prohibits universal truth, or *parallax truth* as we may now call it, rather it is the paranoia and crisis-bound consciousness of open society styled perspectivism (deriving particularity from its constituent Anglophonic and Semitic elements) which impairs higher-order reasoning in service of its own cynicism. Myopic morality declares, *"If I don't do it someone else will"*. Owing to this, myopic morality may as well be synonymous with cynical reason (as an aside: so too does it include its own criticism as a method for disarming opposition, driving the comparison home even further). Eschewing universal (or parallax) truth for raw, dominating political capital is the basis of myopic morality, and simultaneously, the cause of its own defeat as well. Myopic morality (*MM*, henceforth), the morality of neoliberal open society-styled democracy, cannot genuinely step into the universal. It cannot embody the space of truth belonging to another for it is, itself, body-less. While practitioners of *MM* fastidiously study power, seek to know it and emulate it, they can never take the view of power for power is, in its barest essence, hollow and vacuous. "Power" is an oasis in the desert of the deranged mind, driving men constituted by *MM* to their untimely, but perhaps necessary, demise.

Hyperopic morality (*HM*, from now on)—the morality-form which brings us closest to the parallax view of truth—does not eradicate the ego of particularity (the "I" of folk consciousness) but rather builds upon it, curtailing its misguided ambitions and energies while simultaneously extending its depth of perception far beyond the provincial and familiar boundaries which it otherwise calls *home*. *HM* as a cognitive apparatus represents the pinnacle of Man's moral capacity, as it is not only a *sophistication* but also a *unification* of consciousness proper. (Via *HM*, Man's desires are given productive form and expression, thereby moving him further into the mode of virtuosity.) By building upon the ego of particularity rather than negating it (or inflating it, both of which are outcomes of *MM*), *HM* grants man access to a plurality of views, motives, and intentions which may be temporarily embodied for the purpose of furthering his moral education (as well as that of his community). Through *HM,* moral agents come to a relational and teleological view of truth, a necessary advancement in the era of terrestrial globalization where, despite increased calls for transparency (and the occasional *mea culpa* to that effect), the forces which impinge upon Man are ever self-occluding, but more importantly, ever interconnecting.[9] They have a beginning, an origin, as well as an intention. Prejudice—which I have been using in qualified synonymity with *axiom, value,* and *organizing principle*—finds itself rescued by *HM,* discovering a new logical validation which not only preserves its place within those hallowed halls of human cognition, but in fact posits it as both a necessity *and a good* (in the moral sense of the word).

MM recognizes only the "I" of the individual or particularist ego, thereby tolerating only a single authorial interpretation

9 Earlier we affirmed Han's claim that we live in a "transparency society", which remains true despite the seemingly contrary positions taken up here. Supersovereignty remains out of view, that is, the *actually existing* agents of political capital themselves remain in the shadows, while their subordinates (members of the managerial class) operate freely and in full view of the folk population.

(or methodology) of truth, whereas the relationality of *HM* sees the interconnectedness of the many (often rivalrous) perspectives on and claims to the ultimate truth of reality, thus retaining the capacity to situate and interpret truth in its radiant and horizon-expanding fullness. Readers may stop to wonder why such a distinction is necessary to make, or perhaps, what the concrete benefit in adopting the parallax view of truth might even be. Are these concepts themselves even valid? I have not yet fully articulated the meaning and benefit of the parallax view, and so such questions—while arriving too early in the discussion—are nonetheless worth addressing (or in this case, *anticipating*). The great criticism of folkish authority is its supposed predisposition to totalitarianism, but this is only true of folk-authorities which feign allegiance to universal truth (such as the authority of the open society). Authority which operates under the direction of *MM,* folkish or otherwise (though we should admit before proceeding any further of the primal firstness which is often the prerequisite to authorial status) is, itself, the stereotypical or even prototypical form of totalitarianism. In other words, it is the overestimation (or overreaching) of a particular authority, which, in extending itself into ever larger social spheres or spaces, affects a dangerous contamination in discourse and action. Totalitarianism being the political form of foreclosure, *MM*-derived authority suspends all further investigations into truth and knowledge; as interpretation-production is no longer possible under these conditions, so too does *possibility* become impossible. Our reasons for acknowledging (rather than constructing) such a distinction are both ideational and practical. Beyond merely being a blight on the human spirit, *MM* represents the stagnation of consciousness through the means of political organization—it stifles thought, stymies creativity, and arrests development. Worse than any accusation we may level upon it, it is antithetical to life. Even its own.

HM is the cognitive-perceptual form which aligns itself

with the very form of truth; truth(s) are not autistic or atomic, rather they cluster together, living and moving in associations or relations. We may as well speak of *families* (rather than mere *networks* or *associations*) when we speak of the truth. This is the relationality of truth. There is in fact a hierarchy of truth(s), as well, with that arborescent structure conforming to the teleology of truth itself; this structure does not adhere to some man-made principle or institutionally enforced dogma, but rather to the divine origins of truth. As such, we must acknowledge that some truths are "truer" than others, and the meaning of such a thing can only be derived by attuning the mind to their respective relations and directionality.

By declaring one fact, object, or instance as *truer* than another I am simply calling attention to the reality of human action and adjudication, where truth is no longer restricted to endless discursiveness and theorizing. For us as temporal beings, from time-to-time truth must work its way down from the ivory tower of ideation and plant itself deep into the field of human endeavoring. In these moments we seek to maintain the integrity of truth—particularly of our methodologies of truth-seeking—in the face of those all-too-common confrontations with rivals, rabblerousers, and voyeurs alike. That we struggle to do so reveals the ontic reality of our present crisis: rather than characterize it as a crisis of truth, we should identify it as primarily a crisis of *cowardice* (and consequently, those related human failings which skulk around under cover of night along with it, such as indulgence, pity, and self-aggrandizement). Understandable and yet catastrophic all the same, such weaknesses inhibit us from speaking and acting in accordance with respect to our primal situatedness. We thus lose our sacred grounding, and with it, access to the universal dimensions of truth, love, and beauty which rather than *negating* particularities of truth, in fact enhances and extends them. Hence why I emphasize the importance of *meaning* and *interpretation* in adjudicating competing truth-claims or value-statements, for in proclaiming the death of grand metanarratives, we seeded our rightful claim to these crucial devices—devices which enable us to affirm our way of life during this ongoing and deterritorializing period of terrestrial globalization.

Multiplicities beset America with thundering force and speed (as they did the other Western nations of the world): multiplicities of people-groups, desires, technologies, frameworks, and so on, all of which, if administered in isolation would be enough to cripple the native will to live. Confronted by successive waves of multiplicity, these cornerstone concepts (truth, meaning) and devices (interpretation) were altered through critique, polemics, and judicial activism, taking on a wholly new and derogatory character. But this new character is no more factual than what preceded it, rather it is the byproduct of cynical, Manichean reason. Truth's new character (we might better say its new mask) is simultaneously that of an individual whim or frivolity (as in, "*He is just speaking his truth*") while at the same time a force of power, either personal or institutional (as in, "*This is true because I say so, and because I say so it is also true for you, too*"). Under this new mandate, truth is simply yet another vector for the will to power (as Sloterdijk himself has noted of cynical reason). According to the parallax view, however, truth is characterized by *richness*, not *oppressiveness*. "Submission" to the truth is not submission at all, for that only reinforces the notion of truth as a dominating force and as a force of metaphysical colonization. When we speak of submission we really ought to speak of *acceptance* or even *recognition*. Truth is neither a shackle nor an albatross, instead, it is one of the only pure sources of manumission available to us.

Truth ought to be understood as that which *is* and is therefore *unchanging*. It is the *meaning* of truth, however, which expands and recedes according to one's position or relation to it (the forces productive of man's interpretative lens). This is the meaning of the parallax view of truth. We therefore strike upon once more, for the sake of a lasting emphasis, the precise reason why *MM* can never grasp truth in its total complexity and interpenetration: one must be willing to transcend the shortsightedness of ego (without abandoning it entirely) if he is to brave a grander view of reality. Parallax truth is the reward gifted to stewards and torchbearers and the epistemological mode held by visionaries and trailblazers, alike. None of this is to say that *MM* is not generative of creativity or novelty, that it doesn't carve out paths for growth, only that its fruit spoils far faster than those plucked from the garden of parallax truth.

Truth is given its absolute meaning and depth through directionality (teleology), but its *meaning for us* is derived through relationality and context, ultimately culminating (or derivable) through *interpretation.* We, as temporal beings, derive our context through certain material and historical circumstances—this represents the most superficial or perceptible level of our own existence. However, our final, or ultimate, context is derived from our divine origins. Again, this is teleology, which is why I say that *HM* is the cognitive-form of truth itself; it is the psychic mode of the individual and his or her community in alignment with its teleological birthplace. This is the basis, or foundation, of parallax truth.

Let us speak more directly now to the question of meaning and relationality, before moving on to some simple demonstrations of parallax truth. From a given standpoint, any event, interaction, object, *et cetera*, takes on a discrete significance—we might also call this its *meaning*. The position of pure prejudice reifies this specific meaning occurring along whatever plane, field, or context it happens to inhabit or originate from within. We identify this intersection as the basis for an interpretative lens, or at least, the base of interpretation which may be further developed by stepping outside of pure prejudice and into the parallax view. A given interpretative lens may be bolstered by affect or ideology, raising or diminishing (in potential, at least) the scale and technicality of its interpretative analysis, though it must be said, never to that of the parallax view. Irreconcilability and incoherence,[10] our main obstacles (the intractability of which we are attempting to resolve by introducing the concept of "parallax truth"), are not capable of being overcome by pure prejudice on account of its short-sightedness. Pure prejudice, trapped as it is within its own proximality, is ultimately victimized by its overcommitment to particularity: a particular view of history (one's own), a particular view of human nature (rooted and resolved only through violence), a particular desire (unquestioned domination), and a particularly rigid self-concept (defined, often, by a heavily mythologized trauma-narrative). Nonreflective, or un-rescued prejudice renders truth static and subordinates it to its own particular set of historical contingencies and material or social circumstances. This is the most basic level of interpretation available to Man, and the most widely practiced method of interpretation as well.

In effect, we are speaking of a reductionism by the ego which narrows the interpretive field such that truth takes on less meaning, has less interpretative value than it might otherwise enjoy, and consequently, locks the community into a habit of inertia. Nonreflective prejudice has only a single reference, a single point of relationality—itself. As such, it is productive of the lowest forms of meaning-making or truth-seeking.

10 Incoherence arises from defects of the intellect, but also from the structural and methodological inadequacies brought to bear on a given inquiry. Observations, proofs, and conclusions fail to "add up" due to operational and possibly even genetic flaws. This is a relatively less-troubling obstacle, an all-too-human error, for we can always devise better tools and introduce a more competent intellect to the investigation. Irreconcilability, however, is one of the great ailments of our time and the true reason for bringing about the parallax view of truth. The open society's solution to this problem (which has proven an abject failure) was to demote native sovereignty, deny the folk ego (under the guise of ego-death and self "transcendence", and elevate the ego of alien sovereignty – the other). Parallax truth seeks to preserve the folk ego and open a space for it to ascend into a system of universal truth-seeking.

The horizon of meaning which all truths contain is denied in favor of a narrower but more politically useful horizon of expediency. From this dim horizon, that which, at first glance, may appear to us in the form of irreconcilable differences, foreclosures of possibility, or validations of irrational prejudice, may (when perceived from the parallax view) suddenly erupt into deeper and more complex realities which possess the ability to expand folk horizons (expanding them into the horizon of universal truth), thereby opening a new space of movement and interpretation—a new realm of action and conceptualization—which was previously denied to man. Of course, there are times when the fact of reality *is* located within irreconcilability, foreclosure, and inarticulability, and there exists no such interpretive lens or meaning-making mechanism which might alter this condition. This is also the truth of reality. As temporal beings we often find ourselves at an impasse of one sort or another. But possibility, as we have said, is only truly perceptible through those higher levels of cognitive and social development. Parallax truth grants that capacity for discernment which identifies the one from the other (that is, the impasse from the breakthrough).

In speaking of relationality, I am speaking of the individual and his or her "position" (self-assessed or otherwise) in space and time; one's relation to family, faith, and environment—to him or herself—dictate the shape and strength of interpretation applied to some object, locale, or event. This relationality, and as we have said *consciousness* of this relationality, produces its own discourse which then instructs the form (and success) of man's interpretative lens. The health of man's own development informs his relationship to truth itself, to the conceptual and metaphysical realms as well as his immediate social and material conditions, and so impoverishments of his psychological and interpersonal conditions will result in an impoverishment in his concept of truth. As a result, he (or she) will struggle to extract much of anything from any investigation into the depth of life, and of reality, leading him (or her) astray in the discernment of life's moral dimension. If directionality orients and situates us to truth, relationality represents the depth of meaning-making possible to the individual and his or her community. Interpretation gives us the framework for interfacing with discourses of truth, but that interpretation is itself dependent on the principles of directionality and relationality.

What does all this look like then, this parallax truth, whence applied to our present condition? Parallax truth is not Hegelian, in the sense of synthesizing or abolishing the distance between disparate truth-claims (or views of truth). Rather, it is about enhancing the power to produce truth-claims at all. The notion that we live in a "post-truth society" is faulty, for we are in fact living through a period of tyrannical dissimulation: actually-existing political agency obscures itself through its knowledge of mercantile and juridical magic while fortifying this position by hermeneutically altering all discursive currents. Truth is still possible—and powerful—but it now requires a cognitively-derived architectural edifice upon which to stand. A mind-artificed-megaphone from which to address the masses of man.

The parallax view aims toward truth but does not take the creation (or identification) of an absolute truth, as its sole legitimating aim. Certainly, we seek to collapse the asymmetry between rival truth-claims (when and if possible) and restore the possibility of making authentic, competent, truth-claims. Our aim in introducing the parallax view, is to restore teleological thinking, but furthermore, to return agency and authority back to man. Our nature as temporal beings prohibits us from beholding absolute truth on demand, at our whim. Where theorization and discursivity fail, courageous action must intervene. Most times, irreconcilability is merely cowardice, for not all challenges may be anticipated or resolved by the "democracy" of thoughtful speech or Habermasian communicative rationality, but by the "authoritarianism" of a truly ethical willing intention. The parallax view brings us to a place of mutual recognition, mutual self-understanding, but we must also remember that this is not enough. Peace through discursivity is nothing but a liberal phantasy. In fact, the open society acknowledges this; theory and discourse are but two of the tools necessary to affect revolutionary change, the most prolific (not to mention, *pugnacious*) tool is social pressure—physical action undertaken in the arena of first things. The parallax view brings us to a place in which informed ethical action, regardless of its consequences, may finally be possible. (That is to say, it helps us to delineate between actual irreconcilability and simple egoistic pride.) The open society, obsessed as it is with ethics, betrays the fact of its *para-ethicity* by supplanting the presently existing and competently grounded ethical foundation in favor of wild speculation and haphazard experimentation. While we cannot return to that original grounding as it was constituted prior, we can reignite and recontextualize that grounding in service of our present challenges.

"Soft" irreconcilability (as in the impaired reasoning and action of the cognitively dissonating person) may be overcome by the parallax view, for it brings the individual into authentic confrontation between the ontic reality of their actions and the ego-fortifying delusions of their "philosophy". An operation such as this, if conducted within the context of a rejuvenated firstness, can bring the individual back to reason, and ultimately, back to joy. "Hard" irreconcilability, that is to say, the conflicts which emerge due to intra-sociobiological/inter-sociobiological rivalries are—for obvious reasons—more intractable. In postulating the parallax view, I do not assume we can achieve some suspension of temporal law such that "an end to war", "an end to racism", *et cetera*, may ever meaningfully be won. These too are mere liberal phantasies, and while we ought genuinely to seek a diminishment in wanton violence, the pursuit of such an end need not demand self-castration. Through the parallax view it may be possible to dispel phantastical and anti-social ethno-metanarratives, and in doing so enter a space of authentic contact such that inherited historical and existential anxieties may be attenuated. Out of this, an *integral* (as opposed to *instrumental*) rationality may emerge.

We may still answer this question (*"What does all this look like then?"*) more concretely. Life presents us with many commonplace instances which demonstrate the superiority of the parallax view. Consider, for example, the crisis of sex relations and its relation to family formation: the war between the sexes demonstrates the lunacy (and the irreconcilability) of pure prejudice, for the needs of the individual man and woman's ego, hyperinflated and listless as they are, necessarily lead to agonizing contradictions and life-sapping joylessness. Woman seeks self-actualization but splits her "self" in two, stranded in the chasm between the desert of the real (her essential femininity) and a hyperreal phantasy (her transfeminine ideal which seeks conquest). Man, too, seeks self-actualization but is similarly caught amid an externally imposed dichotomy: his desire for authoriality is undermined by the casting of his authenticity into the shadows, while his conscious efforts are freed to pursue to vulgar egotism. The truth of temporality intertwines with the truth of femininity, just as it does with the truth of masculinity, and it is by denying the ontic reality of truth's relatedness—grand truths have brothers, sisters, cousins, and nephews—that Man slips into despair. The truth of love, for instance, presupposes the truths of dignity and integrality: one cannot pursue love while denigrating themselves. The truth of happiness presupposes the truths of loyalty and commitment, and so one cannot expect happiness if he seeks frivolity. The truth of creation presupposes the truths of revelation and authenticity, for without them the created object lacks a proper essence. When man and woman deny the relationality of truth, they deny themselves the very possibility of a joyous life, replete with meaning and purpose. A parallax view of truth would bring man and woman into reconciliation by affirming their essential belongingness, embeddedness, co-enmeshment, and so on. Adopting the parallax view brings both parties to an authentic consciousness of themselves (through which they may discard the falsehoods which hold them back, and begin to live as fulfilled beings).

Conceptual Motility

We have time for one final digression before bringing this analysis to a close, and while this latest detour will not focus on the most critical element of our investigation, it is certainly worth discussing all the same. The end of our investigation brings us back, once more, to that great Hungarian prophet of the open society, Karl Popper, whose system we have very nearly refuted. One aspect of his thinking has escaped our analysis so far, and to that we now direct our attention. Mr. Popper's infamous allergic reaction to definitions and origins was taken up by neoliberal democracy as a mode of indoctrination and of governmentality. Therefore, we cannot understand our present condition without keeping one eye toward the neo-nominalism of open society social engineering (which Popper so enthusiastically advocated).

Whether we look to the crisis of so-called gender identity, or the crisis of national sovereignty induced by replacement migration (just to provide a few examples), we see the social cost paid by America's commitment to the eradication of the universal and the conceptual. No longer can we speak of womanhood, for there are only individual women who are, themselves, constituted in a myriad of arbitrary and conflicting ways. This variegated self-constitution—multiplicities of womanhood as opposed to a standard, or prototype, of femininity—was first secured by the self-skepticism of an authentic liberal tradition, only to be reified courtesy of the deterritorialization (and subsequent reterritorialization) wrought by open society neoliberalism. The same circumstance has befallen our concept of nationhood: while this was affected equally as strongly by the technological shrinking of geographical space *viz* advancements in communication and transportation, propositionality too played a critical role in its elimination. Multiplicity, once more, is the word of the day. Anyone can be an Irishman, for example, and in fact Ireland's folk constituency has always derived itself from multiplicities of the earth's peoples. According, to advocates of the open society, this has been the fact of Ireland's existence all throughout its history—and even though it wasn't, it has all but been formally made illegal to state otherwise.

The first movement destroyed neither conceptuality nor universality; rather, it sought only to provide a new context and justification for which to maintain participation within them (a participation befitting the freshly risen dawn of scientific imperial society). It is with the second movement, however, that the need for replacement-justifications turned malicious. And with that, we arrive upon what I am terming *conceptual motility.*

Conceptual motility (or *CM*) refers to the transformation of all formerly well-understood concepts, definitions, terms, *et cetera*, into completely free-floating signifiers of wholly solipsistic import. This is not to be confused with *concept creep*, defined as the expanding of a concept such that it includes unrelated or only tangentially related phenomena. Conceptual motility describes the practice by which one concept may be substituted for (or even simply associated with) another regardless of their indigenous semantic meanings. Under such conditions, discourse is no longer guided by a process of joint signification or a common understanding. Instead, it is directed by an army of private (and competing) signifieds which may or may not cohere with one another. *CM* is the consequence of Popperian neo-nominalism, as it naturally, *effortlessly*, follows that by abolishing *the* Ideal, one is always left with an endless *number* of ideals, each as "good" or "meaningful" as the next. The ideal is arborescent, authorial. In abolishing the ideal, Man thrusts himself into a vulgar materialism of the flesh, left only with his sense of pleasure and arousal to hold court on those matters which necessitate proper discernment. Conceptuality and ideality, while not exactly synonymous, nonetheless depend quite extensively on one another, as conceptuality allows us to understand and interface with the corresponding instances of representation. Not only does this render Man's perceptual field vulnerable to misinterpretation, but it hinders development of a properly informed teleology of life. In the absence of genuine conceptuality/ideality, we are left with a libidinized cognitive apparatus. Or in other words, a method of self-referential and affect-guided adjudication.

We may yet illuminate this idea further. Consider the following phrase:

"Music is my religion."

I do not doubt that many of you have heard this statement (or something like it) before. To the ear of open society sycophants, this sentence is accompanied by a seductive melodiousness, soothing the neoliberal mind. They hear this sentiment and hypothesize an unjustified serenity and peacefulness of mind. It flatters their naïve and democratic egos. *"Truly, Man is his own master!"* To our ears, however, such a statement is preceded by the kind of cacophony befitting a man or woman governed by an unwell mind.

What does this statement tell us? It tells us that our speaker views the aural pleasure wrought by music as sacral, transcendent. It also tells us that our speaker cannot distinguish between those things which *feel* good or provoke good *feelings*, from those things which *are* good, or which generate *works* of goodness. We can also deduce that our speaker conflates the feeling of being overwhelmed by a given sensation to the feeling (or experience) of divinity. Therefore, we can assume that our speaker is not capable of knowing divine experience, transcendence, sacrality, *et cetera*. He or she may know their simulacra, but no more than that. Our penultimate conclusion, then, is that the individual uttering this statement is both confused and estranged: confused, for the capacity to think in terms of distinct categories is clearly in disarray, but also estranged, for our individual is no longer in touch with a formal (and importantly, *particular*) code of life which would have provided him (or her) with an authentically divine tradition. The final thing this statement tells us is that our speaker has been *fatally* stricken with conceptual motility.

We know that we are dealing with *CM* when we observe an individual (or community) whose existence is dictated by the mutability of terms, and therefore also, the misinterpretation of experience. In much the same way that the presence of a theory allows us to interpret facts, or simply discover instances as being factual (or as containing a latent factuality), concepts allow us to identify experiences, and as such, to interpret them. We cannot have meaning without conceptualization; we certainly cannot have proper ethical action without a functioning conceptuality, either. Human cognitive development depends on the emergence and maturation of conceptual thinking, to which the "fixation" on beginnings and definitions is crucial. And so, while Mr. Popper may have disagreed with the ancient philosopher's penchant for essentials and ideals, we find now that he was not capable of overcoming this tendency in the whole of mankind simply by casting his distaste in philosophic terms. Of course, this did nothing to deter the social engineers of the open society for they, being driven by motivated reasoning and thus wholly disinterested in truth or virtue, sought self-defense and cynical self-advancement, eschewing philosophical rigor in favor of political influence. By *nudging* him, *disciplining* him *piece by piece* and *step by step*, the social engineers of neoliberalism would drive Man into the forms of thought amenable to their own survival.

The ascension (and dominance) of Popperian neo-nominalism hardly suspended Man's need for categorization, rather it retarded his natural inclination to cleave experience into fixed constructions of meaning, which, from the point of view of deterrence of the closed society, was an equally satisfactory outcome. Popper was thereby able to achieve (albeit posthumously) the eclipsing of folk conceptualization by means other than rational discourse: institutional coercion. His perverse focus on the institutionality of liberal democracy would enable later advocates of the open society to take control of conceptual consciousness through education, mass media, and even the state itself.[11] The tiresome charge of "fascism" (and the accompanying horror of being targeted by such a claim) which increasingly accompanies the most banal experiences of daily American life is surely one of the stronger testimonies to this fact. That whole swaths of the population are no longer willing to come to *their own* defense, even worse, that they do not see the open society as itself being a predatory political ecology is even stronger proof.

At this point, the relationship between *CM* and suspicion-culture ought now to be coming into focus, with the challenges posed to the folk account of history by *CM* hopefully now becoming apparent. If we do not control the very terms or grounds for our conceptualization, then we can only fail to understand our own circumstances. History, as with other intellectual trades, therefore, becomes an impossible project. Only the consensist account of history remains, for only the powerful and connected may think (much less think *clearly*).

11 The proliferation of CM allows for the reversal in meaning of simple concepts like "friend" and "rival". It can transform the meaning of kinship into something perverse and dishonorable. Signification is a communal phenomenon, not an individual one, but within neoliberal democracies the community no longer exists and so signification is achieved through a dynamic and distributed arborescence; it is through the hegemony of the open society that signification occurs, but this signification (which is derived covertly and internally) is disseminated via the institutions of liberal democracy.

It is not only appropriate, then, but *necessary* to view *CM* as a political technology designed for the purpose of waging psychological warfare. Its aim? The demolition of executive reasoning. Instances struggle to become aggregates. Because experiences no longer aggregate in the mind as categories (or are miscategorized according to the open society telos), we can no longer reliably interpret experience.[12] As such, there is a constant pouring over and reexamination of *personal* history, to the total exclusion of *world* history and, most significantly, *folk* history. This is easily observed in the now widespread phenomenon of what I am calling here *psychobanalysis*. With psychobanalysis, the individual's mental life is reduced to the constant and solipsistic reviewing, revising, reimagining, and reinterpreting of the facts of daily social life with little mental bandwidth for any other form of cognitive activity or inquiry. Not even the lives or biographical accounts of other, more notable social figures hold sway over individual consciousness as they once did (consistent with hypermodernity's shift to immediacy and self-obsession). Gossiping and rumormongering about celebrities lost its appeal owing not only to the open society's tendency toward self-dissolution (of social conventions and folk identities, for instance) but also because of hypermodernity's tendency toward increased distribution and democratization of celebrity status. The more "society" (a shorthand way of saying here, "the aggregated forces of resource extraction") innovates methods of enticement and

12 Open society conceptuality negates normative conceptual formation in part through the injection of its own anti-concepts. These anti-concepts (which function as a kind of formalized, top-down program of sophistry) obscure concrete realities of human experience *viz* conflation and dilution, as well as through paralogical appeals to non-quantifiable phenomena. Instead of a general factor of intelligence, we have the theory of multiple intelligences. Rather than innate group disparities, we have White supremacy. Any domain or sphere of life threatened by the revelatory light of a rational folk account gets bombarded by open society anti-conceptuality (the occlusion of domains of inquiry through institutional negation).

seduction, the greater the inflation of individual ego becomes. Self-importance (and self-entitlement) are invariably the results of a consumer culture whose most significant social element has become the mere exchange of goods and currencies.

Naturally we are most interested in and stimulated by the facts of our own existence but now, our own existence is no longer characterized by mere banal drudgeries. Or rather, the banal drudgery of the common person's life has been dressed up, glamorized by a previously unknown experience of intrigue. Inquiries into the motives and goals of others, particularly within the realm of politics and mass society, thus descend into the petty intrigue and soap opera drama of the average person's shallow and dissatisfying daily life. There is no longer room for grand political gestures or programs, only professional wrestling levels of narrative complexity. And while that's not to say that characterological barbarity has no bearing on the political, folk accounts directed by *CM* invariably reduce human motivation and interaction to the lowest and most tragic denominator. Under these conditions, folk suspicion-culture in general descends into a play of personalities, each of whom are deterritorialized of any intrinsic character and then transformed into objects of pure projection and raucous, shadow-libidinal fantasy (that is to say, containers for the dark and unintegrated desires of the folk historian, e.g., the Republican obsession with Hunter Biden and his predilection for prostitutes and illicit drugs, among other things).

Hyper-dramatization of the individual's autobiographical discourse predictably follows a liberal framework, and so the individual's mental life comes to be dominated by the discourse of secular psychotherapeutic culture. We speak and think in terms of trauma and abuse, gaslighting and narcissism, trapping ourselves in a minor league mentality of social, and ultimately political, dynamics. Folk suspicion-culture is thus upended by these fixations (on trauma and tragedy, helplessness, and indomitable evil), rather than thinking in less pornographically affective terms. Where it would aid us to think in terms of self-interest, for example, thanks to *CM* we struggle to reason in non-psychopathological terms. We may speak of the irrational non-pejoratively, as in the irrationality of axiomatic prejudice (which serves as a starting point, giving a directionality to folk inquiries) or negatively, as in the case of the non-conceptuality of *CM*; while we must inevitably supplement prejudice with a universal reason (parallax truth), reason can never give aid to the irrationality of *CM*—it can only further distort it. To heal *CM*, we must go back to the beginning of thought and reform the individual's capacity for conceptual thought. A re-education, of sorts, though one that does not come to us accompanied by the usual connotations associated with the word.

By plunging headlong into our own autobiographical history, we lose touch with an arguably even greater history: a history composed of our inherited traditions. Tradition is the great adjudicator and guarantor of history, and without it, we cannot make sense of our present experiences nor substantively access those from our past. The future then, that is *our* future, escapes conceptualization and as such, no course forward may be chartered. A proverbial bridge to nowhere, "the future" (whether as a concept, a destination, or even simply *as a social incentive*) takes the form of a pernicious lie or hoax, as well as a method of coercion or cooption which is only ever deployed in service of returning the individual to his shackles, to keep him slaving away for persons or causes he neither knows nor cares for. Understandably, this too crushes the true joy of life, as the joy of fulfillment (that is, of belongingness, purpose, and a singularity of meaning—themselves only accessible through future-orientation) which is *organically self-sustaining* gets cast aside in favor of inert and self-destroying hedonism.[13] Vulgar

13 Contrast the organic self-sustaining tendencies of closed society social organization with the artificial and economically coercive fortification of the open society. The "joy" produced by open society neoliberalism se-

pleasures (and their pursuit) then become the only meaning knowable—or worth knowing—to the average person. But the hedonic treadmill always shucks off its rider, inevitably casting him into the hell of joylessness. Wherever one looks he sees naught but fleeting moments of euphoria followed shortly by endless rivers of tears.

This buffers the open society *against* folk restoration, for the open society—we might call it by its other name, the *PSoE*—contains the population *viz* the self-affirming inertia of presentism. Only traditions can speak of a future, and thanks to the cynical reason of enlightened neoliberal democracy, traditions are only understood pejoratively. Consequently, the future as a space of hope and fulfillment is forsaken in favor of the future as a space of deception and control. All, shall we call them "futurist" concerns, are thusly subjected to histrionic skepticism, e.g., birth rates, scientific and technological developments, the national debt, and so on.

Life itself is reduced to an endless rush of stimuli and sensations—each as indecipherable and over-stuffed with interpretation-less meaning as the next. The loss (or relinquishing) of folk history thereby gives rise to a dominant consensist history, and along with it the subsumption and overcoding of folk suspicion by *regime suspicion*: a paranoia from outside. Consensist history is in fact an *anti-history*, achieved not merely through by the suppression of authentic folk history but *viz*

cures itself through the strength of the state *viz* its military and economic might, which is to say that it is entirely contingent, relying on the good health of some political engine to sustain it. Transient and destabilizing, it is necessarily a "joy" which comes at the expense of another. Our present predilection for diversity and multiculturalism, for instance, does not occur anywhere of its own volition but because of certain forms of political and economic organization for which the aggregation of multiplicities is *a method* and not *a virtue*. The joy of the closed society, on the other hand, is self-derived: it comes from nowhere else but within that community. It is self-constituting, self-replenishing, and does not require the impingement or enslavement of another to enrich itself.

the reinterpretation of it which serves the strategic aims of contemporary, neoliberal democracy. Through the institutionality of liberal democratic states, the open society makes its own contribution to our present crisis of surplus meaning. *CM* is necessarily propagated by this institutionality, and as such we should consider the practice of *CM* as yet another vector for the production of schizoidal joylessness, but further, as a method of fortifying the consensist account of history.

Abolishing Cynical Reason

Whether we speak of the folk or the community, tradition or history, we are speaking of the same phenomenon: sustained contact with the primal originary, or the ecstatic life, which are the only non-cynical means of self-preservation available to us. A life of joy through purpose and participation, rather than consumption and domination. And especially a life of authentic joy (future-orientation) as opposed to the ameliorating effects on consciousness as produced by vulgar joy (presentism). Authentic joy does not overshadow or overcode our moment-to-moment experiences of life—it simply gives them organization and direction whereas vulgar joy, the joy associated with an eternal "now", forecloses the possibility of a future. (Future possibilities become subordinated to the tyranny of the ever-present moment).

We live and then we die, with large swaths of the in-between acquiring form in one way or another thanks to our nervous fear of death and loss. We cannot afford to dismiss or neglect these facts of existence (e.g., death, pain, loss, humiliation, *et cetera*), and we certainly cannot hope to overcome them. In our attempts to overcome our own temporality we merely make a pathetic mockery of ourselves, and, once again, foreclose future possibilities. Self-preservation is a necessary feature of life, but it is not life's sole constituting dimension. If we are to end the cruel reign of cynical reason, we must learn to transcend the mere need to live. We must not aspire to mere reproduction of ourselves or of our way of life, we must also reproduce the social technologies of ecstasy and joy which make life worth living, and which open future possibilities of beauty and excellence, legacy, and overcoming. Absent the perpetuation of these devices the will to live collapses upon itself, and so in a way, joy and persistence appear to keep pace with one another. Perhaps one is synonymous with the other.

Cynicism makes a monstrosity out of life, to which our creative endeavors are then called upon to slay the beast which terrorizes us. Only we make a critical mistake in adopting this posture: life (and all its pitfalls) is not monstrous; it is only through the panicky lens of death anxiety that life become something we must tame, or if necessary, destroy. We cannot understand our own lives and yet we aspire to create simulacra which will supplant life as we know it? Cynicism is the shortcut to self-ruination.

Sloterdijk proposed a return to the kynicism of Diogenes as a remedy to the stultifying lifelessness of cynical reason, however I am suggesting something both far simpler and far less interested in "the game of philosophy" than that. The return to tradition, or to history—especially as antidotes to cynical self-enlightened neoliberalism—invariably fall prey to reactionary perspectivism, for they only ever amount to a kind of *returning for myself* or a *return to the (psychic) womb*: these are measures which seek a return to a private and autobiographical sphere of utopic complacency. This attitude betrays itself for the open society offers many routes for the strategic recuperation of frustrated social capital, most especially by way of nostalgia. Nostalgia is the great anesthetic of consciousness (revolutionary or otherwise), for not only does it bring the nostalgic individual back to a place of relative comfort, but it also distorts the comfort-object, negating the very practice of "returning" itself. The nostalgic man or woman "returns" to a place that they in fact have never been before, and moreover, that had never existed in quite the way it was imagined having occurred in the first place. Nostalgia, then, is one of the great false consciousnesses of hypermodern neoliberalism.

As we have already noted, to a great many people the future is a farce and the only places left for them to inhabit are either in the present or in the past. The present, however, despite the bounty of pleasures and satisfactions it has to offer, is still experienced as routine drudgery (as evinced by the widespread practice of escapism and self-negation), thus proving to be a competent albeit imperfect anesthetic. Our past, in particular our *autobiographical past*, however, is an eminently mineable resource by which individuals (and their loved ones) may be seduced into capitulating once more to the tyrannical aims of the open society. Fashions always come back into style, new generations always rediscover once-popular musical genres or movements, and the next hit cinematic franchise is always just one reboot away from international acclaim. Each reemergence extends along with it an invitation to submit once more; in the realm of politics, we see this with the return of the tyrant who, having once been roundly condemned rises once more, greeted by the sound of thundering and sycophantic applause. For example, Donald Trump's single term as president saw many ghouls make their fiendish return, chief among them George W. Bush.

The lure of one final hurrah, one more round—for old times' sake—exerts a greater influence than any would care to admit. This past orientation, demonstrative of our self-forgetting as well as indicative of the widely felt experience of defeat, suggests to me that our desire for a return to familiarities and to easy conveniences is destined to fail. What is needed are precisely those things which the outstanding success of liberalism's program of terrestrial globalization let slip from its back pocket during a wild night of conquering and plundering. What is needed is precisely that which mid-century neoliberalism attempted to dispose of more finally, albeit haphazardly. What is needed, then, is a return to firstness, primality, the originary, and the ecstatic. What is needed are those things which the open society's architects freely admitted would be lost the moment we banished closed society-styled political organization and social theorizing.

Those things, the fundaments of identity (commonalities of ethnicity, language, geography, religious practice, and so on), far from being obstacles to either technological or social progress (however one chooses to define such things) are in fact the necessary pre-requisites to all fledgling transformations of the human lifeworld. Importantly, those people-groups must enjoy executive status over themselves and their territories, they must remain authors of their respective discourses and beneficiaries of their individual traditions for without these assurances they cannot know authentic knowledge or creativity. Nor can they know true joy. Absent these social technologies there can be neither progress nor transformation. Even a liberal interlocutor would have to admit such a thing.

The postwar mutation of the world's liberal democracies has clearly led to a rupture, a discontinuity, within the tradition of liberalism. We cannot say that the liberal democracies of Great Britain or the United States of the present year are homologous to those of the previous century. Certain strains have prevailed while others receded, like the ocean the tide rolls in and out, but we allot a certain amount of innovation or dialectical movement within a discourse or philosophical view as part of the natural churn of the creative process. The neoliberalism of 21st century America, however, is like a rabid cannibal willing even to take a bite out of himself. How to account for this? Well, our mutation was not *chemical* but *sociobiological.*

That we have accepted and conformed to the dictates of the open society is not, primarily, because the whole of Western society was swayed by this novel theory of social organization. Rather, it was because unfamiliar and distal people, each with their own history and world picture, were folded into the population of Western countries, altering their new homelands to be more accommodating to them and their needs. The result was what we might term an *ethnogenetic superposition*, or in other words, the production of a new people-group through the merging of formerly distinct and coherent people-groups, leading to a privileging of the subjectivity of one of the constituent elements over the other(s). In the earlier, more conventionally "liberal" period of American history, this privileging aligned with the will and desires of the majority racial stock. Under neoliberalism this mandate was suddenly, violently, reversed.

In most cases, ethnogenetic superpositioning blurs the line of identity, occurring in regions where ethnic and religious identity were synonymous with or identical to national identity, but are now muddled by the sudden inclusion of a radically distinct ethnic (and in many cases, racial and religious) other. With regard to the ethnogenetic superposition (abbreviated as *ES*), intertribal conflicts are reproductively encoded directly into the individual, introducing a historical tension into a people-group which was not previously part of its authentic experience. Such a transformation has consequences for the larger social organism itself, as discursiveness and self-conception (among other things) are irrevocably altered by the introduction of these newer, more disparate elements. From the point of view of suspicion-culture, *ES* introduces a kind of skepticism and paranoia that would otherwise never have found expression among that group. New paranoid strains find their way into the culture, with the competing folk accounts engaged in an ever-escalating hyperbole of conspiratorial ideation and historical revisionism. That neoliberal democracies works to aggressively fortify the ego of their pet constituencies lends a truly distortionary and psychotic narcissism to these novel folk accounts of history.

This newfound abundance of people-groups naturally contributed to our surplus of meaning, specifically an overinflation in the meaning of ethnic and national identity. Suddenly it became plausible for a man who was born in Nigeria, and who lived a substantial portion of his life *as* a Nigerian *in* Nigeria, and who later emigrated to Ireland to declare himself, now, *an Irishman*. Similarly, a first generation Jewish-American woman born to a pair of Hungarian refugees may take it upon herself to relitigate the American Civil War and agitate for reparations or some other slavery-related social cause despite only setting foot in the country some hundred years later, thereby lacking any direct or ancestral experience with that tumultuous period in the country's history. With *ES* there can be no interpretation, only excoriation and vilification.

And yet this appears to be the outcome advocates of the open society *prefer*. It seems that the open society *prefers* unmitigated resentment, cascading wave after cascading wave of suspicion, and the over-proliferation of every kind of domestic rivalry possible: between differing races, religions, classes, generations, and as well between the two sexes, all in service of the cynical self-preservation of neoliberal democracy. Well then, definitionally speaking, the open society is, itself, anti-progress for it stakes its survival on the demolition of the very forces which generate meaningful social and technological progress. Here we see again the fruits of cynical reason: securing one's future comes gleefully at the expense of everyone else's well-being. To bring an end to *this* iteration of suspicion-culture, mend the paranoid minds of some four hundred million Americans, and forge a path toward authentic and eusocial progress requires but a single sacrifice. To free ourselves, we must exit the open society.

Glossary of Technical Terms

Aperioristos — Greek, meaning "limitless" or "absolute".

Arthurianism — A hypothetical model of human action and sovereignty which is properly teleological.

Atrocity of Power (AoP) — Denotes the undesirability, or unenviability of true power. "True power" being defined as the capacity to transform or transcend. In effect whenever we speak of "power" we intend "agency", which speaks to the capacity to act and will freely. The greater one's capacity to act, the more "powerful" he is.

Concept creep — The process of expanding a concept beyond its intended semantic meaning, to the point of uselessness.

Conceptual motility — The degradation of conceptual thought into free-floating signifiers; neo-nominalism.

Cynical Reason — 20th century German Philosopher Peter Sloterdijk's term for the Enlightenment tradition of skepticism.

Ethnogenetic superpositioning — The process by which two identity-groups merge, privileging the dominant identity-group over its supplicant.

Faustianism — Oswald Spengler's term for the European tendency toward self-overcoming.

Folk account of history — A substitutive term for the more commonly understood phrase, "conspiracy theory".

Hyperopic morality — A teleologically informed cognitive apparatus.

Kynicism — The Greek philosophical tradition embodied best by Diogenes.

Madness of reason — Intended to denote the capacity for narrow-minded, reductive, and monomaniacal thought when over-privileging logos.

Myopic morality — A non-teleologically informed cognitive apparatus.

Neo-Real (nR) — A substitutive social order which overcodes normative eusocial behaviours towards some artificial intent.

Originary Order — The order of a given tradition or society prior to desacralization.

Parallax view of truth, the — A methodology of truth-seeking.

Permanent State of Exception (PSoE) — The undeclared indefinite suspension of normative and organic standards, conventions, expectations, and laws in service of an aspect of the State against its totality.

Politics, Hot — A McLuhan-esque framework for revolutionary or radical politics which is defined by its tendency towards being high-definition, low-participation, and detribalizing.

Politics, Cold — The low-definition, high-participation, and retribalizing mode of politics native to the SoE.

Power — The accumulation of means (productive forces).

Reason of madness — Denotes the alien and eccentric logic (an actual, though imperceptible to most, logic) of the schizophrenic, the mystic, the poet — or in other words, the irrationalist.

Simulacrum — A duplicate or otherwise replicated object or system.

Spectacle, the — 20th century French philosopher and sociologist Guy Debord's term used to describe the social phenomenon whereby that which was previously lived can now only be experienced as a representation. Debord attributes this decline to the outgrowth of "commodity fetishism".

State of Exception (SoE) — 20th century German philosopher and jurist Carl Schmitt's notion of a state, event, or condition, which precedes a temporary extra-legal intervention by the State in defence of itself.

Suspicion-Culture — The forces generative of (and in turn, generated by) paranoia, fear, and skepticism.

Totalitarian Imperial State (TIS) — Any political territory which operates through outward expansion and inward repression.

Bibliography

Alper, Sinan. 2021. "There Are Higher Levels of Conspiracy Beliefs in More Corrupt Countries." PsyArXiv. May 20 .

Alper, S., & Imhoff, R. (2022). Suspecting Foul Play When It Is Objectively There: The Association of Political Orientation With General and Partisan Conspiracy Beliefs as a Function of Corruption Levels. *Social Psychological and Personality Science*, *0*(0).

Apollodorus, Library, Sir James George Frazer ed., book 3, chapter 15, section 8.

Archive Author. "Wide Distribution of Anti-Semitic Material Reported in Massachusetts." *Jewish Telegraphic Agency*, March 7, 1962. https://www.jta.org/archive/wide-distribution-of-anti-semitic-material-reported-in-massachusetts.

Asai, T., Sugimori, E., Bando, N., Tanno, Y., (2011). "The hierarchic structure in schizotypy and the five-factor model of personality", *Psychiatry Research*, vol. 185, Issues 1–2, pp. 78-83.

Bentall, R.P., Claridge, G. and Slade, P.D. (1989). The multi-dimensional nature of schizotypal traits: a factor analytic study with normal subjects. *British Journal of Clinical Psychology*, 28, 363-375.

Berkowitz, Reed. "A Game Designer's Analysis of QAnon:

Playing with reality", Medium. September 30, 2020. https://medium.com/curioserinstitute/a-game-designers-analysis-of-qanon-580972548be5.

Blaauw, Elien M. n.d. "The Association between Maladaptive Personality Traits and Belief in Conspiracy Theories." Uvt.Nl. Accessed August 10, 2023.

Brotherton, R., French, C.F., Pickering, A.D., (2013). "Measuring belief in conspiracy theories: the generic conspiracist beliefs scale", *Frontiers in Psychology*, vol. 4, pp. 1-15.

Bruder, M., Haffke, P., Neave, N., Nouripanah, N., & Imhoff, R. (2013). Measuring individual differences in generic beliefs in conspiracy theories across cultures: Conspiracy mentality questionnaire. *Frontiers in Psychology*, 4(225).

Christopher Bollyn: The Man Who Solved 9/11. "n.d. www.bitchute.com. Accessed June 16, 2023. https://www.bitchute.com/video/ToFwgxHIo93P/.

Cicero, *De Natura Deorum* II, 28 (32), quoted in Wagenvoort, Hendrik (1980). *Pietas: selected studies in Roman religion.* Leiden, NetherlandsL Brill.

Claridge, G., McCreery, C., Mason, O., Bentall, R., Boyle, G., Slade, P., & Popplewell, D. (1996). The factor structure of 'schizotypal' traits: A large replication study. *British Journal of Clinical Psychology*, **35**, 103-115.

Clifton, Jon. "The Global Rise of Unhappiness". *Gallup*, September 15 2022, https://news.gallup.com/opinion/gallup/401216/global-rise-unhappiness.aspx.

Coady, David. *Conspiracy Theories: The Philosophical Debate.* p. 13-15. (New York: Routledge, 2018).

Crocker, J., Luhtanen, R., Broadnax, S., & Blaine, B. E. (1999). Belief in U.S. Government Conspiracies Against Blacks among

Black and White College Students: Powerlessness or System Blame? *Personality and Social Psychology Bulletin*, 25(8), 941–953.

Douglas, Karen M., Sutton, Robbie M., Cichocka, Aleksandra. "The Psychology of Conspiracy Theories." *Current Directions in Psychological Science* 26, no. 6 (2017): 538–42.

Douglas, Karen M., Uscinski, Joseph E., Sutton, Robbie M., Cichocka, Aleksandra, Nefes, Turkay, Ang, Chee Siang, and Farzin Deravi. "Understanding Conspiracy Theories." *Advances in Political Psychology 40*, no. S1 (2022): 3-35.

Elia-Shalev, Asaf. "How an ADL spy operation helped bring down the far-right John Birch Society". *The Times of Israel*, May 21 2023. https://www.timesofisrael.com/how-an-adl-spy-operation-helped-bring-down-the-far-right-john-birch-society/.

Frantzman, Seth. "Was the Russian Revolution Jewish?" *The Jerusalem Post,* November 15 2017, https://www.jpost.com/magazine/was-the-russian-revolution-jewish-514323.

Friedman, R.A., (2021). "Why Humans Are Vulnerable to Conspiracy Theories", *Psychiatric Services,* vol. 72, issue 1, p. 3-4.

Galliford, N., & Furnham, A. (2017). Individual difference factors and beliefs in medical and political conspiracy theories. *Scandinavian Journal of Psychology*, 58, 422–428.

Georgiou, N., Delfabbro, P. H., Balzan, R. (2021). "Could autistic traits be a risk factor for conspiracy beliefs? An analysis of cognitive style and information seeking behavior.", *Minerva Psychiatry*, vol. 62, no. 4, pp. 231-240.

Goertzel, Ted. (1994). "Belief in Conspiracy Theories", *Political Psychology,* vol. 15, no. 4, pp. 731-742.

Gonçalves, André, Gabriel Franco, Gabriel Vitor Gomes, Gisele Machado, Giselle Pianowski, and Lucas de Francisco Carvalho. 2022. "Personality and Adherence to the COVID-19 Vaccine: The Role of Agreeableness and Openness Traits." *Archives of Psychiatry and Psychotherapy* 24 (1): 13–21.

Green, R., Douglas, K. (2018), "Anxious attachment and belief in conspiracy theories", *Personality and Individual Differences,* vol. 125, pp. 30-37.

Grzesiak-Feldman, M., & Irzycka, M. (2009). Right-wing authoritarianism and conspiracy thinking in a Polish sample. *Psychological Reports*, 105(2), 389–393.

Hagen, Kurtis. (2018). "Conspiracy Theorists and Monological Belief Systems", *Argumenta, vol.* 6, p. 303-324.

Hart, J., Grather, M., "Something's Going on Here." *Journal of Individual Differences*, vol. 39, no.4, Oct. 2018, pp. 229-237.

Hayden, Brian. 2018. *Shamans, Sorcerers, and Saints*. Smithsonian Institution.

Hill, Faith. 2023. "America Is In Its Insecure-Attachment Era." *The Atlantic*, April 27, 2023. https://www.theatlantic.com/family/archive/2023/04/insecure-attachment-style-intimacy-decline-isolation/673867/.

Hofstadter, R. (1965). *The Paranoid Style in American Politics, and Other Essays* (New York: Knopf).

Huebner, Robin. "North Dakota Link to Notorious Son of Sam Murders Part of New Netflix Documentary." InForum, May 17, 2023. https://www.inforum.com/news/the-vault/north-dakota-link-to-notorious-son-of-sam-murders-part-of-new-netflix-documentary.

Imhoff, R., Bruder, M., "Speaking (Un-)Truth to Power: Conspiracy Mentality as a Generalised Political Attitude." *Europe-*

an Journal of Personality 28, no. 1 (2013): 25-43.

It Wasn't about Oil, and It Wasn't about the Free Market: Why We Invaded Iraq." 2015. In These Times. February 11, 2015. https://inthesetimes.com/article/what-the-iraq-war-teaches-us.

Keller, Morton (2007). *America's Three Regimes: A New Political History*. New York, NY: Oxford University Press.

Kusters, Wouter. 2020. *A Philosophy of Madness*. MIT Press, p. 165.

Laing, R.D., *The Divided Self* (Tavistock Publications, 1959), p. 112.

Lehmann, Chris. "We All Live in the John Birch Society's World Now". *The New Republic*, November 23 2021. https://newrepublic.com/article/164510/live-john-birch-societys-world-now-robert-welch-biography-review.

Leone, L., Giacomantonio, M., Williams, R., Michetti, D., (2018). "Avoidant attachment style and conspiracy ideation", *Personality and Individual Differences*, vol. 134, pp. 329-336.

Little, B. (n.d.). *How America's First Third Party Influenced Politics*. HISTORY. https://www.history.com/news/third-party-politics-anti-masonic.

Martinez, Anton P., Shevlin, Mark, Valiente, Carmen, Hyland, Philip, and Richard P. Bentall. "Paranoid Beliefs and Conspiracy Mentality Are Associated with Different Forms of Mistrust: A Three-nation Study." *Frontiers in Psychology* 13, (2022): 1-11.

McLuhan, Marshall. (1994). *Understanding Media: The Extensions of Man*, First MIT Press Edition (Massachusetts Institute of Technology).

Miller, J. M., Saunders, K. L., & Farhart, C. E. (2016). Conspiracy endorsement as motivated reasoning: The moderating roles of political knowledge and trust. *American Journal of Political Science*, 60(4), 824–844.

Monacelli, Steven. "The John Birch Society Sees a Renaissance in North Texas". *The Texas Observer*, July 21 2022. https://www.texasobserver.org/the-john-birch-society-sees-a-renaissance-in-north-texas/.

Mulloy, D.J. (2014). *The World of the John Birch Society: Conspiracy, Conservatism, and the Cold War* (Tennessee: Vanderbilt University Press).

Oliver, J E., and Thomas J. Wood. "Conspiracy Theories and the Paranoid Style(S) of Mass Opinion." *American Journal of Political Science* 58, no. 4 (2014): 952-966.

Ovid, *Metamorphoses*, (Oxford University Press, 1970) Book XIII.

Parsons, S., Simmons, W., Shinhoster, F., Kilburn, J. (1999). "A test of the grapevine: An empirical examination of conspiracy theories among African Americans", *Sociological Spectrum*, vol. 19, issue 2, pp. 201-222.

Piper, Michael Collins, *False Flags: Template for Terror* (America First Books, 2019), Ch. 29.

Rabinowitz, Howard N. (March 1988). "Nativism, Bigotry and Anti-Semitism in the South". *American Jewish History* 77(3). pp. 437–451. The Johns Hopkins University Press.

Raihani N.J., Bell V. (2019). "An evolutionary perspective on paranoia", *Nature Human Behavior*, vol. 3, pp. 114-121.

Richey, S. (2017). A birther and a truther: The influence of the authoritarian personality on conspiracy beliefs. *Politics & Policy*, 45(3), 465–485.

Skinner, B. F. (1947). "Superstition' in the Pigeon," *Journal of Experimental Psychology* #38 .

Sloterdijk, Peter. (1984). *Critique of Cynical Reason*, translation by Michael Eldred; foreword by Andreas Huyssen (Minneapolis: University of Minnesota Press, Theory and History of Literature; v. 40) Original: *Kritik der zynischen Vernunft*, 1983.

Smithsonian Magazine. "How the 19th-Century Know Nothing Party Reshaped American Politics." *Smithsonian.com*, Smithsonian Institution, 26 Jan. 2017, https://www.smithsonianmag.com/history/immigrants-conspiracies-and-secret-society-launched-american-nativism-180961915/.

—— (2019) *Conspiracy theories abounded in 19th-century American politics, Smithsonian.com*. Smithsonian Institution. Available at: https://www.smithsonianmag.com/history/conspiracy-theories-abounded-19th-century-american-politics-180971940/ (Accessed: February 22, 2023).

Stasielowicz, Lucas. (2022). "Who believes in conspiracy theories? A meta-analysis on personality correlates", *Journal of Research in Personality*, vol. 98.

Suspect in 1974 Stanford murder case contemplated suicide before (2018) *ABC7 San Francisco*. Available at: https://abc7news.com/san-jose-shooting-murder-stanford-memorial-church/3677065/ (Accessed: 08 June 2023).

Teixeira, A. R., Valdiney Veloso Gouveia, V. V., Soares, A. K. S., Moizéis, H. B. C., 2021. "Crenças Em Teorias Da Conspiração Em Estudantes Universitários: Uma Explicação a Partir Dos Traços de Personalidade." *Psicología Conocimiento y Sociedad* 11 (2): 84–98

The Economist. "Conspiracy Theories Are Dangerous—Here's How to Crush Them." *The Economist*, August 12, 2019. https://www.economist.com/open-future/2019/08/12/conspiracy-theories-are-dangerous-heres-how-to-crush-them.

"The Philadelphia Nativists Riots". *irish-society.org.* Archived from the original on 2002-11-20. Retrieved October 21st, 2023.

Tron, Gina. "How The 'Son Of Sam' Terrorized NYC And The Evidence That Led To His Capture | Oxygen Official Site." Oxygen Official Site, May 4, 2021. https://www.oxygen.com/true-crime-buzz/how-david-berkowitz-terrorized-nyc-victims-evidence.

Uscinski, J. E., & Parent, J. M. (2014). *American conspiracy theories.* New York, NY: Oxford University Press.

Uscinski, J. E., Klofstad, C., & Atkinson, M. D. (2016). What drives conspiratorial beliefs? The role of informational cues and predispositions. *Political Research Quarterly*, 69(1), 57–71.

van Prooijen, J.-W., Krouwel, A. P. M., & Pollet, T. (2015). Political extremism predicts belief in conspiracy theories. *Social Psychological and Personality Science*, 6(5), 570–578.

van Prooijen, J.W., & Douglas, K. M. (2017). "Conspiracy theories as part of history: The role of societal crisis situations". *Memory Studies, 10* (3), 323–333.

Vlamis, Kelsey, n.d. "Rep. Marjorie Taylor Greene Said 'like a Lot of People' She Had 'Easily Gotten Sucked into Some Things I Had Seen on the Internet' Regarding QAnon Conspiracy Theories". Business Insider. https://www.businessinsider.com/marjorie-taylor-greene-got-sucked-into-qanon-conspiracy-theories-internet-2023-1.

Weimar Republic (1918 – 1933) - Yad Vashem. the world holocaust ... Accessed June 3, 2023. https://www.yadvashem.org/odot_pdf/Microsoft%20Word%20-%207794.pdf.

Printed in the USA
CPSIA information can be obtained
at www.ICGtesting.com
CBHW041240110224
4169CB00002B/3

9 781923 104143

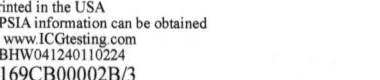